MW01171207

Learning to be a Good Editor

by Adapting Novels into Screenplays, and Stage Plays

Ava Collopy

Thank you to friends, family, artists of inspiration, and to readers of mine.
I hope you find what you're looking for.

Introduction

I don't consider myself as being an expert on all the in's and out's of writing but I thought this was a very interesting approach, and for me it was the one that really made me understand how to edit prose. So I figured I may as well pass on what I learned to the great universal pool of writers and other creative types and hopefully it will prove useful to someone.

   Enjoy.

Chapter 1—The Practice (what you Learn from Adaptation)

Trying to learn how to write screenplays made me a better prose writer. It made me edit my novels with visuals, dialogue, and minimalism in mind, which made them better books. As they say, to be a good writer you must be a great editor.

I began of course by reading a few screenplays and novels adapted into screenplays. I found *The Talented Mr. Ripley* and *Strangers on a Train*, both by Patricia Highsmith, and both turned into movies by renowned directors, particularly useful. I saw what parts of the stories were removed and what was changed.

Amazingly, the *Ripley* movie is an extremely rare instance where the film is better than the book. This is because of one simple change: in the book Margot and Dickie are close friends but in the film they are engaged. That one simple but important change makes the whole story better. It adds a great deal more tension and emotional involvement and intensity.

In *Strangers on a Train* a key thing was changed to make it better for telling a story with film; Guy's job was changed from architect to tennis player. This didn't make the story better, per sé, just better for a film. In the novel his job as an architect works fine but would have been pretty dull in a film. Making him a tennis player added an athletic dimension and was a great way to create tension; he has to win a tennis match, and quickly, as he must rush off immediately afterwards.

In both of these adaptations very little of the stories is lost. However, due to the size of the books, a lot is often lost in adaptations to film. One example *East of Eden*, originally written by John Steinbeck, where the whole start of the story, where we see the troubled mother, has been cut out.

One of course has to view and read these and other adapted stories to get their own sense of adaptations.

When *Eat, Pray, Love*, a nonfiction book by Elizabeth Gilbert, was hugely successful, like any reasonable writer, I investigated it to see why it was so popular. I watched the movie and read the book… until the author's constant chatter made me throw the book across the room in frustration. I don't think I could have written a screenplay out of that book. There was simply too much in it. To do it would involve trying to hone in on only a few of her major points, but there are many life lessons and experiences covered in it, and a great deal of incessant chatter, much of which is only somewhat relevant to what is kind of a central story about giving herself permission to be her own person and pursue her own path.

Additionally, much of what she experiences and learns is very internal. I think it must have been an unenviable task for the screenwriter to try to figure out how to communicate all of that visually.

After studying enough of others' works I went to my own to adapt one of my novels into a screenplay. One of the major differences between prose writing and screenwriting is that with prose word count is the main focus, whereas with screenwriting page count is the main focus. This is because one page, properly formatted, is considered about one minute of screen time. Also, instead of Times New Roman font you use Courier, which takes up more space. The exact details for formatting either prose or screenwriting can be found elsewhere, like on the internet. I'm far more concerned with the process.

The experience of trying to turn your own novel, that you poured your heart, mind, and soul into, into a screenplay is very, very difficult. For my novel *8 Days a Week*, which is a family drama, I would, for example, have large sections with the family's back story. I played around with the idea of doing

1

flashbacks but very quickly ran out of space. It was at first very hard to cut large sections of a story I worked so hard on out, but eventually I found it very freeing.

When back story had to be put in I used short pieces of dialogue to say a lot with as few words as possible. I quickly determined that flashbacks would be very cumbersome anyway. I preferred to keep everything in the now, especially as this challenged me further. It would have been too easy for me to turn the back-story into flashbacks—and then overshoot on the space by 50 pages or so!

8 Days a Week is normally about 99 pages and 62,150 words. In Courier font with proper screenplay formatting it's more than double that. And generally a screenplay isn't supposed to go beyond 110 pages—just under two hours of screen time. There was, evidently, a lot to cut out.

This process actually helped me to re-edit the last chapter and make it much better. Much of the story is very insular, taking place in Sean's internal monologues but in the last chapter his life has improved. So, after having the experience of adapting the story into a screenplay, I thought I should use more dialogue in just that last chapter to show that improvement. It worked to great effect, bringing that chapter more to life and really demonstrating the improvement in Sean's life.

With screenplays you're supposed to show and not tell. So I had had to change a lot of the narration into dialogue for the screenplay adaptation. After I was finished I took some of the screenplay adaptation and put it back into the novel as I was getting ready to publish it. (I wrote, edited, and published *8 Days* when I was still a landscaper and handyman's assistant largely to make a point about the wasted potential in the working class.)

Editing *8 Days* was very hard because, like any artist, I was very emotionally attached to my creation. But the editing process made it a much better manuscript. As I couldn't afford an editor I asked several writer and reader friends of mine to be "test readers" and provide feedback. Some gave a little feedback and others wrote notes throughout. I took the advice and edited it accordingly. The original handwritten and then typed manuscript was about 72,000 words. And when I first wrote it I would have told you nothing could be cut out.

Turning it into a screenplay wasn't just a matter of cutting out words but thinking in a totally different way; how to change it to dialogue, how to create more motion, how to say a thing without saying it directly.

This is very hard to do as a writer, especially because it involves cutting up your own work, but it's also very invigorating because you change everything from a narrative into pure action; what's happening *now*, what they're doing *now*, what they're saying *now*. It feels very awake and alive. Some depth and meaning is lost, but that also leaves a lot to be created by the reader's (or viewer's) imagination.

It's an invigorating experience for a writer and I would recommend it to any writer, especially as it teaches you a great deal about editing, which is largely just the ability to stop being overly emotional and sentimental about your own writing. It also teaches you to be less "psychotherapeutic" about things; less focused on things that happened to your characters in childhood or their teen years, and so forth and much more focused on everything happening in the here and now. I think this is a good exercise for us as people anyway since modern Western society is very preoccupied these days (and has been for quite a while now) with constantly dragging up the past and making people relive old wounds.

The best way for me to explain the transformation from prose to screenplay though is to use the screenplay technique of not telling you but showing you. So below is an unchanged excerpt from *8 Days a Week*. Then what follows later in this book is the same part of the story changed into a screenplay. For the

Learning to be a Good Editor ~ Ava Collopy

full effect you'd obviously have to read the original book, but this will give you an idea of what I'm talking about.

EXCERPT 1: Chapter 1—The End of the Workday

The air grew colder as the sun set in the dark gray sky. When the wind picked up it felt like frost was biting at his arms, cheeks, ears, and nose. He put a jacket on over his wool shirt as he leaned out of the driver's seat of the dark blue two-door Ford pick-up truck while writing an invoice. His cousin loaded their two gas-driven push lawnmowers onto the gunmetal gray trailer with the paint flaking off of it.

He tried to do some creative writing with the invoice like he used to do when he had essays to write in school. He stretched out each word to make it longer and taller than it needed to be and included in it each individual task he could think of: Lawn mowing, weed control, edging, fertilizing, moss killing, then he paused trying to come up with anything else he could add onto the bill to get the price up. After a minute or two of thorough concentration he concluded that that was all he could put on the bill, so he wrote et cetera for effect. Then he wondered how much he could get that particular customer to pay for all the work he and his cousin had just done for the past hour.

He would have charged $200 if he could have gotten away with it but he settled for putting $65 on the invoice instead. He took a deep breath and blew it out forcefully to alleviate the tension of not knowing if upping the price would displease this customer, and wishing he could just keep upping it. His cousin opened the passenger side door and got into the truck and they both closed the doors in a vain attempt to banish the cold.

"It's getting cold out there Sean," his cousin said.

"It sure is Alan," he said then added, "I had to put on my jacket while I was writing the invoice."

"I'll bet you did."

Sean put the invoice book down on the seat between the driver's and passenger's seats and pulled his red and black checkered thermos off the floor, unscrewed the top, and poured himself a nice hot cup of coffee into the cup that the top of the thermos made.

Alan pulled his turquoise thermos with the silver top off of his side of the floor and poured himself a nice hot cup of tea.

"Ugh!" Sean said. "I don't know how you can drink that stuff. I can't even stand to smell it."

"What, tea? I thought you liked tea."

"I like *black* tea; not *Earl Grey* tea. It has that disgusting almost floral scent and flavor to it. It just grosses me out."

"Oh really?" Alan said with a smile that suggested a mixture of amusement and irritation.

Alan took a big sip of tea then exhaled dramatically to spread the scent of it around the cabin of the truck as much as possible.

Learning to be a Good Editor ~ Ava Collopy

     "Ugh! That's disgusting!" Sean said, half joking. "I'm going to have to deliver this invoice right away just to get away from that awful smell," he said with a smile.

[The full novel is available on Kindle Unlimited for $0.00 and regular Kindle for $4.99 here: https://www.amazon.com/Days-Week-Story-Working-Novel-ebook/dp/B019CKXP3C/ref=sr_1_1?keywords=ava+collopy+8+days+a+week&qid=1693165772&sr=8-1]

     Notice the formatting: new paragraphs and lines of dialogue are indented five spaces, dialogue is in quotations, there may be italics for emphasis, you need to really work at describing the details of the characters and the scene because otherwise there's no visual, and so on.
     Contrast this with screenplay formatting, including that dialogue is in blocks, indented at about 11 to 42 spaces in, under a character's name in ALL CAPS, and brevity is key. A screenplay is more like poetry in that way. But the thing you'll probably notice most of all is the shift to sheer immediacy and minimalism: the bare, essential story in the now.
     The full adaptation will follow, but for now just look at how much it changes on the first page:

```
FADE IN. EXT. A NICE NEIGHBORHOOD - MIDDLE / UPPER MIDDLE CLASS - LATE
DAY

Two men working on a yard; mowing, edging, putting lime on it, etc.
They are cousins, SEAN FLANAGAN and ALAN FLANAGAN. Sean is about 49,
Alan is about 51. They look tired, worn down, but Sean looks more
ragged. When their work is done Sean writes in an invoice book while
Alan finishes putting the mowers, etc. away in their work truck and
trailer. It's so cold Sean has to put another jacket on as he leans out
of the driver's side seat. After a while Alan joins him and they close
the doors.

INT. SEAN'S TRUCK - LATE DAY

                    ALAN
          It's getting cold out there Sean.

                    SEAN
          It sure is Alan. I had to put on
          my jacket while I was writing the
          invoice.

                    ALAN
          I'll bet you did.
```

     As you can see, this new format of telling a story is actually a whole new way of telling a story and requires almost an entirely new way of thinking altogether. And that becomes the real trick of this type of adaptation. It's all still in the same language: English, but it is not in the same "writing language". You

Learning to be a Good Editor ~ Ava Collopy

have to change how you think about the story, how you approach telling the story, in order to effectively adapt your story from one format to another. Each has a different head space and different pros and cons about doing the work in that way, pros and cons to communicating in that other writing language. So it's not just about learning a new format, it's about learning a new language.

I'd compare it to some of my experiences trying to teach myself some Spanish; if I take a Raphael song and translate the lines word by word I may or may not understand what I'm looking at. Sometimes I can know what each individual word means but not understand the sentence because the way it's said in English is totally different. If I then take the full line and pop it into Google Translate it will give me not really the exact translation but the way we say the same thing in English. To understand Spanish I'm seeing that I need to rethink how a sentence must be structured. So, for example, in "Escándalo" he says: "No me interesa que te tome por sorpresa" /
"No [negative word] me [me] interesa [interest] que [what] te [you or to you] tome [take] por [for] sorpresa [surprise]" /
Direct translation: "No me that to you take for surprise" /
How we say it in English: I'm not interested in taking you by surprise".
Learning a new writing language can be just as disorienting.

For adapting the work into a stage play, in a class, I was constantly told drama was the watchword. That's why that version of the story has an added scene with the mom Sadie and the eldest daughter Becca. It really gave the actors in the class something to do and created more emotion and tension then Sean hearing about their argument after the fact. It was a good experience as well, but very challenging.

I tried to adapt my other novels but found it much harder. The more I researched the screen industry, which had at first just sounded like fun, and pretty exciting, the less I was interested in it. But I still found this to be a great way to learn how to edit your own work, even if you have no interest in the screen industry. In my experience it really does teach you how to take an outside view of your own work and then tell the same story with as few words as possible. It's good to see how much you can cut out without really losing anything.

One of the main things that I noticed when adapting my novel in stage writing and screen writing classes was how quickly people wanted to get into the drama between the characters. Anything that really brought their interactions to life became a main focus. So I'll show you another excerpt from the novel and then you can see in the adaptations how it changed.

It's interesting to note that in the novel all of the scenes are centered around Sean; there are no scenes without Sean, as it is his story. But when we got into adaptations, a new scene emerged between the mother Sadie and the eldest daughter Becca that isn't in the original and which brought more drama to life in the work.

The experience of changing your story is makes you learn the most, which is why this book is set up to help lead you to have the confidence to just boldly adapt your own work. You will learn the most through experience and shouldn't spend too much time fearfully planning how you might do that. Instead, I encourage you to simply take the plunge and experience it for yourself as that is truly the best way to learn.

EXCERPT 2: End of Chapter 1 and start of Chapter 2—At Home with the Wife and the Eldest Daughter

Learning to be a Good Editor ~ Ava Collopy

[Watch how the work changes from the original prose format…]
[End of Chapter 1]

He pulled into the driveway and dreaded the cold he'd be walking out into. He was glad that he'd been able to fix the truck's heater that summer since he hadn't had heat in his truck the previous winter. He stepped out of the truck and walked a few paces to where he'd left an old rusting wheelbarrow that morning. He rolled it over to the truck, put all the groceries in it, and pushed it up the long, narrow, bumpy, winding, overgrown pathway up to the cabin as two large black dogs barked wildly and tugged at the ropes tied to trees that kept them from running off and nearly getting killed on the highway. He rolled the wheelbarrow up the ramp to the front porch, which was plagued with white patches of dry rot, and left it in the night drizzle. He walked over to the dogs and gave them attention. "Hi Merry, hi Sherry," he said, smiling.

The front door opened and a woman in stretchy, waistless pants stood there with her arms crossed over her ample and sagging chest.

"Hi, Sadie," he said.

"Why do you have to get the dogs riled up every night?!" she demanded. "And god—don't leave the groceries on the porch where they'll get wet and ruined! What is wrong with your brain?!"

"They're under the roof."

"They're under the roof," she said in a mocking and irritated tone of voice. "Becca," she said, leaning into the cabin, "come put the groceries away."

[Start of Chapter 2]

Sean left the dogs and walked to the porch as Becca came out, and they brought the groceries through the front door and the doorway into the kitchen that had yet to have a door put in. The walls in the kitchen and most of the cabin had exterior wallboards with tarpaper stapled on the outside but no exterior siding, and they lacked insulation and dry wall.

Becca was a tall slim young woman with straight black hair, just like her prodigal biological father. The other two kids had average builds with straight dirty blonde hair like Sean. Sean knew it irritated Sadie to no end that all three of her children looked more like their dads than her, with her thick figure that was prone to weight gain and her dark auburn, curly hair.

Sadie brushed the frizzy mess around her head back with her hands hopelessly and sat down at the kitchen table, waiting for Sean to make himself a fresh pot of coffee and pour himself a cup while Becca became a part of the scenery putting the groceries away. He knew that the moment he sat down Sadie would have some complaint just as she did every night. Vaguely he recalled that growing up he'd heard that women were good cheerleaders. He found that odd since many of the women he'd known had only been good at finding faults and complaining. And Sadie certainly never greeted him with any comments like, "Wow, thanks for working hard all day, good job."

[And then the screenwriting format…]

EXT. CABIN PROPERTY - NIGHT

The foliage is dense but you can just make out two mercury vapor lights on the property and the lights of a large cabin some ways into the

Learning to be a Good Editor ~ Ava Collopy

property. He gets out and zips his jacket up. He grabs a wheelbarrow and wheels the groceries up the long hill to the cabin. There are some raggedy dogs outside. He leaves the groceries on the porch and goes to pet them. The front door opens. A woman in her late 40's comes out. She is SADIE; overweight, has let herself go. Her arms are crossed over her chest; she's very unhappy.

                SEAN
   Hi, Sadie.

                SADIE
   Why do you have to get the dogs
   riled up every night?! And god—
   don't leave the groceries on the
   porch where they'll get wet and
   ruined! What is wrong with your
   brain?!

                SEAN
   They're under the roof.

                SADIE (mocking)
   They're under the roof.

She turns and calls back into the cabin.

   Becca, come put the groceries
   away.

Sean leaves the dogs and walks towards the cabin.

[It continues here, with a scene with a lot of family drama; this scene came alive when I actually had people performing it; people really loved it. Watch how it changes in the later adaptations and how an additional scene, without Sean, between the mother and eldest daughter came out of the collaboration of adapting the work with performers around. It was a great experience and I highly recommend it because others can help you to see what in your work will really come to life and what in your work you can get more out of by playing the characters with/against each other more.]

He avoided her as long as possible then decided to face whatever was going to come from her. He sat down and she immediately said, "Do you have any money?"

"No. I didn't get to check cashing today."

"You didn't get to it? Yeah, sure, and what exactly were you doing that was so important you didn't get to it?" Sadie said with a decisive look in her eyes that said she thought he was masking his covert true intentions. "And why do you always come home so late? You say it's not a plan but it must be because you always get home at about the same time every night and—what is *that*?!"

Learning to be a Good Editor ~ Ava Collopy

she said looking at something Becca was about to put away in one of the cupboards that was missing a front door. "That's not VitaMax!"

"They were out of VitaMax. This is the same thing."

"It is *not* the 'same thing' Sean—I did research on the different multivitamins and I…"

As Sadie continued Becca quietly walked across the room to stand directly behind her mother, then she soundlessly mouthed *blah, blah, blah, blah, blah, blah,* before pretending to choke herself. Sean smiled. Sadie turned around to see Becca standing there with her arms by her sides and an innocent smile on her face.

"Why don't you go to bed?" Sadie asked.

"But this is entertainment," Becca replied with a grin. "It's better than the soaps. It's *believable.*"

"Go to your room."

"I'm almost 18 mom, you can't send me to my room—we've been over this."

"She has a point there Sadie," Sean said with a smile.

"Don't *you* step in, you're not even her real father." Sean and Becca immediately frowned and lowered their heads silently. After a long moment of silence Sadie said, "Now Sean, will you be going to church with us tomorrow?"

"I can't, I have to work."

"I can't believe this. Your kids never see you anymore. You're always working seven days a week."

"It feels like eight days a week, and I'm no happier about it than anyone else is."

"Well the kids and I are going. Becca will be singing in the church youth choir, remember? I can't believe you're not going to be there for her."

"I would love to be there but I need to put food on the table."

"She'll be hurt if you miss her performance."

"Yeah well she'll really be hurting if she hasn't got any food to eat or a roof over her head. Just take the tape recorder and the camera."

"We don't have any batteries for them."

"What do you mean you don't have any batteries? I just bought a ton of batteries."

"You bought batteries two months ago."

"Yeah, two months ago I bought a ton of batteries. You couldn't have used them all up already."

"God, you're impossible Sean. You're so damn cheap. You just expect everything to last forever so you won't have to spend any money on anything, ever."

"I'd spend money if I had any money to spend."

"Then why don't you make more money?"

"Well that's why I'm going to work tomorrow."

Sadie threw up her arms theatrically. "I can't listen to you anymore," she said and left the room as Becca rolled her eyes.

"Don't worry about my performance dad, I'm only doing it because mom wants me to, okay?" she said quietly.

"Okay, kiddo."

"I'm going to go to bed," she said and walked out of the kitchen.

"That's not a bad idea," Sean said under his breath. He set his coffee cup down on the table, turned off his percolator, and turned off the kitchen light as he left the room.

Learning to be a Good Editor ~ Ava Collopy

[Here we go into more detail about the space of the cabin where they live. In prose you have these self-indulgences of words. In screen or stage writing minimalism is best. Further, it's the director's decision what the whole scene/stage will look like. And in Hollywood or "Hollywood", your story will get changed a great deal in most cases so it's best to just accept that going into it if you do get a film deal. This chapter has some of his/the family's backstory, which you'll see in the adaptations I simply had to cut out. This is very hard to do when it's your own beloved work but you must learn to be a cold editor and simply cut out everything that does not suit the new format. I found this hard at first and liberating later. And it's interesting that when you don't define much of the backstory the viewers/readers will start to fill it with their own ideas of how the characters got to this point.]

In the front room, near the wall between the front room and kitchen, there was an old metal wood stove with a long rusted metal chimney pipe leading out through the wall. Sean walked over to it and quietly damped all the air vents off for the night. Then he looked around the stove: there were metal baskets of wood drying on top of the stove but nothing looked like it had been there long enough to catch fire, there was plenty of dry kindling by the stove to start a fire with the next day, and the cast iron pot that sat atop the back of the stove had water simmering in it, putting moisture back into the parched air. Sean looked at his knuckles. It was only October and already his hands were drying out. He would have to remember to pick up some kind of salve for them. Every winter the skin on his knuckles would dry until it cracked and bled a little as the skin split open.

Near the wood stove there was a large fluffy couch that was brown, and it was brown with good reason—Sean had picked it up several years before, knowing it would be hard for any dirt to show up on a *brown* couch. He walked the few feet over to the couch and folded it down flat. He took three sleeping bags from a nearby small chest of drawers and threw them onto the couch. Then he took off his shoes and laid down on the couch, under the three sleeping bags, which he laid opened on top of him like blankets. It was too warm for him under the three sleeping bags now but during the night the temperature in the cabin would drop by about 15 degrees Fahrenheit and he would thoroughly need those covers.

He closed his eyes and tried to drift off to sleep but found his mind full of thoughts about church, choir, religion…

Sadie had been raised Baptist, an upbringing that she'd thoroughly rebelled against after moving out of her parents' home. One of the things Sean had liked about her when he'd started dating her was her free-thinking analysis of religion; she used to say it was a tool that kings and emperors had always used to control the masses and make them want to control themselves, "god" being something of an ever-present judge or sheriff making the masses believe that all of their actions, even those they did in the privacy of their own homes, was being carefully scrutinized by others, by "holy beings". When they'd first been dating they would sometimes talk about all the ways in which religions had been used to control people, societies, world events. Sadie had seemed brazenly intelligent to him at that time: a totally independent, freethinking woman with control over herself and the course of her life. But as soon as Brian had been born she'd been talking about baptizing him.

Sean had been raised to see child raising as the woman's domain—not that he believed women *had* to have and raise children, it was just that he'd never been taught what men were supposed to do with children, besides going to a job every day to make the money to feed and house them. So he'd left the raising of the children up to Sadie. Except for this.

Learning to be a Good Editor ~ Ava Collopy

He'd been raised with a religion—Catholicism—that he'd always found very oppressive and he'd watched good young women, like the first serious girlfriend he'd ever had, breaking down and crying in church because they thought they were sinners and priests playing along with it just to make more money for the church. He'd had one very strong opinion about how his children were going to be raised: NO RELIGION.

This had led Sadie on one of her many research frenzies and before he'd known what was happening she'd been dragging him, Becca, and their infant son to a "Unitarian Universalist" church. He'd never heard of the Unitarian Universalist Association of Congregations before then and he hadn't cared to go to any church services but Sadie had been on one of her new project highs and it was much easier to just cave in and go with her on it than to try to argue with her.

When he'd heard and seen their religious service he'd been shocked; the assistant minister had been an out gay man who'd read a short essay he'd written about the continuing human rights movement in their congregations, the struggles of gays, people of color, women, the working class, and how the UU's had always been a welcoming, accepting congregation that supported the rights of all individuals. Then the head minister, a woman from the U.S. South, had delivered a sermon she'd written about hate crimes and how religion often played a role in fostering hatred towards different groups of people. Then the entire congregation had joined hands to sing from the UU's interdenominational book of hymns and words of wisdom.

The UU service had been nothing at all like the starched stiff services of his Catholic youth that told congregants what to think and encouraged everyone, even small children, to be incredibly quiet and reserved at all times, even after they went home.

After the UU service there had been a social hour in the basement, which had been a virtual sea of activity, with about 500 of the 1,000 congregants circulating around. Many of the members had recognized by his more socially conservative nature that Sean had been raised Catholic, and he'd recognized which of them had been raised Catholic as well. But he'd also met many liberal Christian UU's from various sects of Christianity, two people who considered themselves Buddhist UU's, one Jewish UU, and some children who only knew UUism.

Sean and Sadie had talked to some of the children separate from their parents to get a real sense of what it was like for children to grow up with UUism. They'd been so pleased that they'd picked up two enrollment kits from the front lobby that same day. Sadie had voiced an interest in joining the UU's as soon as she could; Sean had sat back and read through the enrollment kit thoroughly, in the same way he'd watched his mother read through important documents when he was a kid.

He'd once watched his mother read through a house contract, and even though she'd only had a ninth grade education she'd been able to find a few faults that the highly educated professionals who'd written and proofread the contract had completely missed. By virtue of his mother's consistent diligence he had learned to carefully read through every last word of anything he was considering signing his name and reputation to.

He'd found that members of the Downtown Unitarian Church of Portland were expected to tithe 10 percent of their annual earnings to the church, in addition to putting money in the collection baskets every Sunday. Then it had become painfully obvious to him exactly why the church had been talking about trying to get new members, particularly more from the working class: they were a predominantly white, upper middle class church that had no concept of the financial struggles of the working class.

Sean had pointed this out to Sadie but she'd joined the church anyway. When it had come time for her to pay her annual membership fee he had told her no, they simply did not have the money. He'd told her she should tell the church that they didn't have that kind of money so maybe they'd learn that that kind of a requirement was impossible for most working class people; he'd also suggested that they might accept volunteer work for the church as payment. Sadie had just gotten mad at him and refused to have contact with that church again so she wouldn't have to, as she said, be embarrassed by his refusing to spend money.

Then she'd started going to the much smaller Willamette Valley congregation, in southeast Portland. He had gone there once for their first Sunday of the month potluck. Sadie had brought one of her moist organic cakes and Sean had brought his appetite. With only 100 people in the congregation it had been easier to socially integrate into the group than it had been at the downtown church.

Sean, Sadie, Becca, and baby Brian had sat at a table in the roomy basement discussing the woman minister's sermon about the importance of sex ed in children's education and how the UU's had an Our Whole Lives mentor to help kids with the transition into adulthood, which had given him hope for the UU's again. After a while though he'd begun to realize that no one was *really* talking about the issue. That no one in UU congregations ever really talked about issues, they just made generalized statements like "sex ed for young people is good". But were they pro-choice he wondered. He'd seen some posters for Planned Parenthood, the National Organization for Women, and NARAL Pro-Choice Oregon in the basement of the Downtown Unitarian Church but there had been no informational pamphlets about those charitable organizations and there had been no one collecting donations for them either. When he'd thought about it he actually had no idea what any UU really thought about birth control, premarital sex, or abortion. Everyone in those churches was just politely dancing around real opinions.

They were good people though and he'd been confident that his children wouldn't be indoctrinated into any one way of thinking while in a UU church so he'd thought it would at least be a good, safe environment for them. He'd seen the UU children running around in the basement, playing, making noise, and other childlike things that no child would ever dare do in a Catholic church. It seemed like a good environment for them, and he couldn't deny that there were some positive aspects to having a church in one's life; it was a social center, not entirely unlike the dance halls and roller skating rinks that had been very popular when Sean had been growing up. He'd wondered what had happened to them. Somehow they'd vanished without a trace when he wasn't looking and there weren't any social centers left, except for churches. But he still didn't care to go to church every Sunday himself.

When he'd been a kid he'd woken up at 5 a.m. every Sunday morning and had been out the door before anyone else in the house had been awake. He'd fed his German shepherd Merlin then fed his pet chickens before running off down the street to the Powell Butte Nature Park. He'd been playing for as long as he could before one of his brothers would come find him, as always, and force him to go back to the house, wash up, and put on his best clothes for Sunday mass. After so many years of working so hard to avoid church he couldn't see himself *willingly* going to church, more than once in a great while anyway.

But Sadie had been able to tell her Baptist mother and Lutheran father that she'd joined a church and would be taking her children to church every Sunday. She'd also told her parents that Sean was refusing to go to church every single Sunday as if he were breaking some law by choosing what to do and what not to do with himself in his own life. Sadie's mother had just said, "What do you expect? He's a Catholic, they can do anything they want if they just confess it later and do a few Hail Mary's."

He'd still gone to the Sunday service once in a while to keep a relationship with the place and the people…and to participate in that delicious first Sunday potluck. Then one day he'd been

Learning to be a Good Editor ~ Ava Collopy

talking about Darwin's brilliant observations with one of the senior members of the congregation, an older woman who was always very encouraging of new people coming in. He'd thought he was finally going to get a *real* conversation with one of the UU's, then she'd made a comment about how she and him were basically better than most of the other people in the church because after all they both had college degrees.

He'd said, "Actually I only got through about two years of college before I ran out of money since I was paying my own way through it. I don't have any degrees." She'd said, "Oh!" and suddenly leaned away from him with a slightly bewildered look in her eyes that confessed a combination of fear at having exposed her true self and disgust at having compared herself to someone she then saw as a sort of lesser life form. Then she'd made up some excuse about having to check on something in the basement kitchen. He had never set foot in a UU church again.

The scars Sean bore from having grown up in poverty ran deep. He remembered being a blissfully ignorant kid playing in the woods with his brothers and cousins, running home to his mother serving dinner and his dad coming home to wash up with Sean and the other boys for dinner. He'd felt completely secure in his home and his family.

Then when he was six he'd been invited to the birthday party of a friend of his, Johnny, who'd lived near Powell Butte too, but in a somewhat nicer neighborhood. Sean had gone to a thrift store with his own bottle return money to pick out a really good gift for him.

Johnny had been a popular kid in the neighborhood and a lot of other kids were going to be there. Sean had carefully looked through the bins of the nearest thrift store to find a good gift. He'd bought a Batman action figure that he actually would have liked to keep for himself. When he'd gone to the birthday party he'd seen that everyone else had been able to buy Johnny brand new toys. The other kids had insulted his gift a little because it was "cheap". Johnny had just seemed a little confused by it and had moved on to the other presents quickly.

That was the first time Sean had realized there were different social classes. That was the first time he'd felt that he was seen as inferior to those around him because he and his family had less money. He'd left the party early, claiming he had a tummy ache and had meandered home slowly, not wanting to tell his parents how the party had gone for him. After that he'd avoided certain parts of Powell Butte just so he'd be sure never to run into anyone who'd been at Johnny's birthday party.

Later he'd been going to Trinity Catholic middle school where there had been a very strict dress code that had created an environment with greater equality than regular public schools. He'd looked as presentable as any other student there and had had the opportunity to be treated better than the students who had financially wealthier parents by his choosing to be a very reliable student who always did his homework assignments and never acted out in class. He'd had good grades and had gotten along pretty well with everyone, fellow students and nuns alike. Most of the kids with financially richer parents had gotten their wrists slapped with a ruler many, many more times than he had. At Trinity he'd been judged for being rich in good character and high standards, without regard for his social class, which had made sense considering that the nuns themselves had taken vows of poverty. He'd done very well at Trinity, but he'd never gone to any of his fellow students' birthday parties, or any parties for that matter.

Then there had been his high school, Barton Polytechnic Trades, an all-boys school where you had to watch your back so you wouldn't wind up getting punched or held upside down from a third story window. He'd managed to make no enemies but no real friends either. He hadn't even been able to hang out in the cafeteria because his family couldn't afford to pay for the food, or the bus.

He'd bicycled to and from his high school and made his own peanut butter sandwiches for lunch every day, which he'd eaten alone outside, not wanting to advertise how poor he and his family were.

The money he'd made at the tire shop where he worked all day every Saturday had gone for schoolbooks and new clothes. He'd never asked his mother for any extra spending money. She'd been working as a maid since his father died. He used to find her tucked away in some little nook of the house crying her eyes out, something that she never did in front of anyone. His mother had been a very emotionally reserved person who as far as he'd known had never cried before his father's death. His father's death had hurt her more than she would ever say, so Sean had tried never to ask her for anything. He'd just bicycled to school every day, eaten his homemade sandwich, done his homework assignments, worked at his job, and dreamed of going to college and maybe becoming a millionaire some day, and maybe offering some grants for kids who'd be struggling as he had. That was back when he was still hopeful.

Finally his mind rested and he was able to drift into a deep sleep.

As you will see in the adaptations, and especially if you read the whole original novel first, as I did with several film adaptations, a work that you had heretofore seen as only able to exist one way can in fact be more like a Modernist work; (as one of my English professors in university in Europe used to say) it's the difference between a perfect mirror image and the image from a fractured mirror, where there are multiple angles and perspectives. I hope you enjoy the read, and see through the examples how it works, then try it with your own work to experience it for yourself.

Chapter 2—8 Days a Week: the novel Adapted into a Screenplay

8 DAYS A WEEK

Adapted from the Novel by Ava Collopy

FADE IN. EXT. A NICE NEIGHBORHOOD - MIDDLE / UPPER MIDDLE CLASS - LATE DAY

Two men working on a yard; mowing, edging, putting lime on it, etc. They are cousins, SEAN FLANAGAN and ALAN FLANAGAN. Sean is about 49, Alan is about 51. They look tired, worn down, but Sean looks more ragged. When their work is done Sean writes in an invoice book while Alan finishes putting the mowers, etc. away in their work truck and trailer. It's so cold Sean has to put another jacket on as he leans out of the driver's side seat. After a while Alan joins him and they close the doors.

INT. SEAN'S TRUCK - LATE DAY

>   ALAN
>   It's getting cold out there Sean.
>
>   SEAN
>   It sure is Alan. I had to put on
>   my jacket while I was writing the
>   invoice.
>
>   ALAN
>   I'll bet you did.

Sean puts the invoice back in the book, has a cup of coffee from his warm-colored thermos; Alan has a cup of tea from his cool-colored thermos.

>   SEAN
>   Ugh! I don't know how you can
>   drink that stuff. I can't even
>   stand to smell it.
>
>   ALAN
>   What, tea? I thought you liked
>   tea.
>
>   SEAN
>   I like black tea, not Earl Grey
>   tea. It has that disgusting
>   almost floral scent and flavor.
>   It just grosses me out.
>
>   ALAN
>   Oh really?

Learning to be a Good Editor ~ Ava Collopy

Alan takes a big sip and exhales dramatically to spread the scent around the cabin of the truck.

                    SEAN
          Ugh! That's disgusting! I'm going
          to have to deliver this invoice
          right away just to get away from
          that awful smell.

They smile at each other.

EXT. MS. BARRINGTON'S HOME - DUSK
Sean exits the truck with the invoice in hand and walks up to the customer's front door. He's slouching, looks exhausted and cold. He rings the doorbell, stands up straighter, puts on a smile.
A woman of about 55 who is a little overweight, MRS. BARRINGTON, answers the door.

                    SEAN
          Hello Miss Barrington.

                MRS. BARRINGTON
          Mrs. Barrington, Sean. Or Ms.
          Barrington now that Joe's gone
          and passed away last year.

                    SEAN
          Oh no, you've got to start going
          by Miss again so you can start
          dating those young 35-year-old boys.

Sean smiles.

                MRS. BARRINGTON
          Oh, Sean Flanagan.

She says as if he's hopeless but she smiles. He hands her the invoice.

                    SEAN
          Listen… I did a few extra things
          on your lawn today because I saw
          that the moss was trying to take
          over again.

                MRS. BARRINGTON
          Oh was it? I thought we killed it

Learning to be a Good Editor ~ Ava Collopy

                    last year.

                              SEAN
                    Yes we did, but it comes back
                    every year.

                              MRS. BARRINGTON
                    Oh, really?

                              SEAN
                    Yeah, that's why I keep treating
                    it very year.

She puts on her glasses, strains to read the invoice, his sloppy
handwriting. She gives up.

                              MRS. BARRINGTON
                    Oh why don't you come in a minute
                    and warm up while I go and get my
                    checkbook.

                              SEAN
                    Thank you.

INT. NICE MIDDLE-UPPER MIDDLE CLASS HOUSE - DUSK

                    I'll close the door for you to
                    keep the heat in. We're not
                    heating the great outdoors, is
                    what my dad always used to say.

                              MRS. BARRINGTON
                    Oh mine too. Mine too. And
                    thanks for being so considerate.

She gets her checkbook.

EXT. MS. BARRINGTON'S - DUSK

He walks out of her house with a check in hand, smiling, walks back to
the truck.

INT. / EXT. SEAN'S TRUCK / EAST PORTLAND - NIGHT

Sean drives them from a nice, middle / upper middle class part of town
into the poor, rundown side of town.

Learning to be a Good Editor ~ Ava Collopy

                    ALAN
Are you sure you want to take
39th?

                    SEAN
I'm going to take 39th to
Holgate, and Holgate to 122nd
—it's the fastest way to get
back to your house.

                    ALAN
I don't know about that. I
would have taken Burnside to
122nd.

                    SEAN
How would that be any faster?
Burnside stalls after the I-205
freeway because of the MAX light
rail.

                    ALAN
It might not be faster but it
would be easier.

                    SEAN
That wouldn't be any easier.

                    ALAN
It would be to me.

                    SEAN
But you're not driving.

                    ALAN
I prefer 122nd in case I want
to stop at the Safeway grocery
by the corner of Powell.

                    SEAN
Why do you ever want to stop at
Safeway—it's overpriced.

                    ALAN
It's not overpriced.

                    SEAN

Learning to be a Good Editor ~ Ava Collopy

WinCo and Fred Meyer both have
lower prices. It's overpriced.

                    ALAN
The items I get aren't overpriced.

                    SEAN
All of the items in Safeway are
overpriced. You can't be getting
the only items in the whole store
that are at a reasonable price
when all of the items in the store
are overpriced.

                    ALAN
Maybe that's what you think.

                    SEAN
That's what I know.

Silence befalls. Alan is irritated but can't argue. After a while Sean
turns off to Foster Road, not Holgate (at 63rd).

                    ALAN
What are you doing?

                    SEAN
I thought we might want to eat
at the Evergreen Diner. I don't
know about you but I don't have
the energy to cook anything at
home.

                    ALAN
I know I don't want to cook
anything at home but won't
Sadie have anything for you at
the cabin?

                    SEAN
I still have to get the groceries
and drive out to the cabin. I
won't be home for another two or
three hours. Besides, I don't
know if she will or she won't.
Sometimes there are dinner

               leftovers and sometimes there
               aren't.

                     ALAN
               You'd think she could leave you
               some dinner since you're paying
               for everything.

                     SEAN
               Yeah, you'd think.

                     ALAN
               You should really talk to her
               about that.

                     SEAN
               And say what? No, it would just
               cause trouble and I'd probably
               wind up looking bad in front of
               the kids and I don't want that.

Silence. Alan is irritated. Just before 72nd Sean pulls into a parking
lot. The Evergreen Diner.

EXT. PARKING LOT / DINER - NIGHT

They walk into the diner, not holding the door open for each other.

INT. DINER - NIGHT

The place is a typical American diner, with Chinese decorations added
after the fact. It's small and crowded. There's a bar-type counter and
a few tables and booths. At the counter there are a few other workmen
and a waitress, CARA, who has dark brown hair, light vacant eyes, a
nice if absent smile, and dresses too colorfully for Oregon (she's from
Florida).
Sean and Alan walk in and pause. One of the workmen sees them and moves
over so they can sit next to each other. They nod their thanks to him,
sit down, wait a second and when they're not handed menus they just
take them from behind the counter. The waitress is distracted: watching
the TV mounted on the wall or chatting with a customer.

                     CARA
               Hi, did you guys just get here?

                     SEAN AND ALAN
               Yes.

                    CARA
          Would you like some coffee?

                    SEAN AND ALAN
          Yes.

                    CARA
          Okay… oh, I'll have to go get
          some coffee cups.

She walks into the back of the diner. Sean gives Alan a knowing look.

                    SEAN (quietly)
          Good ol' Cara.

It takes Cara longer than it should to return with the cups. She sets
them down in front of Sean and Alan and pours their coffee.

                    CARA
          Do you guys want cream or sugar?

                    SEAN AND ALAN
          No, none for me, thanks.

Cara begins to walk back to the back room.

                    SEAN
          Uh—we'd like to order our meals.

                    CARA
          Oh, okay.

She takes a pad and paper out of her apron.

                    SEAN
          Yeah, I'd like pork chops and
          a baked potato with vegetables.

                    ALAN
          I'd like ham and a baked potato
          with vegetables.

                    CARA
          Oh, okay guys.

Learning to be a Good Editor ~ Ava Collopy

She takes down their orders and disappears into the back room again. Sean sees she didn't notice a guy at the end of the counter wanted more coffee. He picks the coffee pot up and gestures to the men next to him. They pass the coffee pot down. They all smile at each other; they like her.

As they wait for her to return they all stare at the TV with glazed-over eyes; too tired to really focus. They're watching *Star Trek: The Next Generation*, the episode where they traveled back in time and met Samuel Clemens.

Cara returns later and serves their food, smiling, then stops to watch the TV and smile like a kid at it. Looks down, smiles.

> CARA
> Oh, so that's where the coffee
> pot went.

> SEAN
> I'd appreciate a refill.

> CARA
> Okay.

She picks it up and disappears into the back room.

> MAN AT COUNTER
> It sure is getting cold out there.

> OTHER WORKMEN
> Yep, Sure is, That's true, Does
> this every year, etc.

EXT. DINER / THE CITY - NIGHT

Sean and Alan walk back to the truck and drive away. Sean drives a few more miles through rundown, working class suburbia to a very average house and yard. It's fenced in. They begin to exit the truck.

EXT. / INT. ALAN'S HOUSE - NIGHT

> ALAN
> Why can't you ever park straight?

> SEAN
> I parked straight, it's the yard
> that's crooked.

Learning to be a Good Editor ~ Ava Collopy

Alan goes to the light gray mailbox that should be white. Gets the mail, looks through it as Sean unlocks the gate. Pets two average-sized dogs, careful not to let them out.

> ALAN
> Hmm, nothing but bills.

> SEAN
> I'm surprised PGE hasn't started
> billing us for the fact they have
> to bill us. (To the dogs) Hi
> Carrie, hi Barry.

Alan walks to the front door, opens it, goes to the kitchen, opens cans of food, feeds pets as Sean goes in and turns off the radio they left on to make it sound like someone was home. Sean sits at the phone table, checks messages.

> SEAN
> Dohring wants to see us this
> next Thursday for some general
> things on her property.

Alan puts food dishes down for Carrie and Barry.

> ALAN
> Do you mean next week or the
> week after next week?

> SEAN
> Next week—next Thursday.

> ALAN
> Then you should have said this
> Thursday.

> SEAN
> This next Thursday.

> ALAN
> This Thursday.

> SEAN
> In any event we've got to be
> there.

Sean gets up, walks about ten feet into the kitchen to make a pot of coffee.

>   ALAN
>   I noticed you got a new
>   coffeemaker.

>   SEAN
>   Yes. I found it at Finders
>   Keepers the other day. I
>   found three actually but only
>   two of them were in good enough
>   condition to buy. I took the
>   other one up to the cabin. It's
>   a percolator as you can see.

>   ALAN
>   Like we grew up with.

>   SEAN
>   Exactly. See, I haven't had a
>   strong effect from the coffee
>   for quite some time now and I
>   ran into a man in WinCo on the
>   breakfast aisle a while back who
>   reminded me that modern
>   coffeemakers don't heat the water
>   or the grounds as hot as the old
>   percolators did and I realized
>   that that was a part of the
>   problem with the coffee these
>   days. Ever since then I've been
>   looking for percolators so I can
>   get the full effect of the
>   coffee.

Alan listens to Sean's coffee monologue as intently as one might listen to a groundbreaking philosopher.

>   ALAN
>   That's good but I'm going to
>   stick to tea.

Alan turns, makes tea.
Sean and Alan sit at the kitchen table. A third seat is empty (Sean's mom's). They look at the empty chair, look away, avoid it.

Learning to be a Good Editor ~ Ava Collopy

Outside a female neighbor comes stomping down the street in high heels
sobbing. They duck back from the window to hide as she passes.
Later Sean is refilling his thermos. Walks to the front door.

                    SEAN
          See you tomorrow.

                    ALAN
          You're coming in tomorrow?

                    SEAN
          I have to. I have five mouths to
          feed, and all the pets. People
          abandon their pets out there. I
          know I can't afford them but I
          can't turn them away.

                    ALAN
          I know how that goes. See you
          tomorrow.

                    SEAN
          See you tomorrow.

Sean walks out.

INT. / EXT. ALAN'S HOUSE / SEAN'S TRUCK / THE CITY - NIGHT

Sean unhooks the trailer and locks it to the fence with a long chain.
Wraps a chain through the mowers and locks that. Enters his truck and
listens to classical music as he drives across town on 122nd.
Everything is pretty run down; strip malls, a strip club, etc. He goes
to Winco. He does the grocery shopping; cheap but healthy foods like
oats, apples, pancake mix, etc. Then he waits through a very long line
to check out. You bag your own groceries. He puts the groceries in the
truck and starts driving home.
He drives from rundown suburbia to an area filled with hideous new,
low-rent apartments filled with slackers: druggies and those that have
babies solely to get welfare and don't care about their kids, nearly
let them run out onto the road.

                    SEAN (under his breath)
          My tax money at work.

FLASHBACK

Learning to be a Good Editor ~ Ava Collopy

Sean remembers playing with Alan and other kids in the same area when it was still undeveloped.

PRSENT. EXT. / INT. SEAN'S TRUCK / THE CITY / THE HIGHWAY - NIGHT

Sean looks at it all again, is appalled. He drives a long way; from suburbia into the countryside, past small farms, and eventually into an area that's just forests. It gets darker and darker, eventually there are no street lights. As he drives he looks wearier and wearier.
At one point if he keeps driving straight and doesn't turn with the road he'll crash right into a big Doug Fir tree. He stares at it and is clearly thinking about it. Then a car honks its horn because he's too far into the next lane so he adjusts, turns with the highway.

                  SEAN (V.O.)
          Keep calm. Becca's almost 18,
          Brian is 15, Devona's 12. In six
          more years she finishes high
          school, then she can work. It's
          just six more years. Just six
          more years.

He continues driving on the long, dark highway. Eventually a cop pulls him over.

                  SEAN
          I wonder what this guy wants.

Sean takes his thermos, drinks a cup of coffee. Then rolls down his window. A man of about 30 leans onto the driver's side windowsill.

                  SEAN (blowing out coffee scent)
          Yes sir, how may I help you?

                  COP #1
          Wow! I thought you might be
          drinking but I guess not.

                  SEAN
          No, sir. I never drink and drive.

                  COP #1
          Okay. Good night.

The cop walks back to his car.

                  SEAN

They stop me almost every night.
They must have some kind of
quota they have to make.

Sean waits for the cop to leave then pulls out and continues. After a
while it starts pouring down rain so hard he can hardly see the road.
He pulls over, looks at the clock on his dashboard.

Sean opens his eyes, it's 20 minutes later. He dozed off.
He gets back to driving. A few miles later he pulls off the main
highway to a two-lane side street and about three driveways in. He
pulls into the driveway of a large, forested property.

EXT. CABIN PROPERTY - NIGHT

The foliage is dense but you can just make out two mercury vapor lights
on the property and the lights of a large cabin some ways into the
property. He gets out and zips his jacket up. He grabs a wheelbarrow
and wheels the groceries up the long hill to the cabin. There are some
raggedy dogs outside. He leaves the groceries on the porch and goes to
pet them. The front door opens. A woman in her late 40's comes out. She
is SADIE; overweight, has let herself go. Her arms are crossed over her
chest; she's very unhappy.

                    SEAN
          Hi, Sadie.

                    SADIE
          Why do you have to get the dogs
          riled up every night?! And god—
          don't leave the groceries on the
          porch where they'll get wet and
          ruined! What is wrong with your
          brain?!

                    SEAN
          They're under the roof.

                    SADIE (mocking)
          They're under the roof.

She turns and calls back into the cabin.

          Becca, come put the groceries
          away.

Sean leaves the dogs and walks towards the cabin.

                                                              27

Learning to be a Good Editor ~ Ava Collopy

INT. CABIN KITCHEN AND FRONT ROOM - NIGHT

The cabin in unfinished. Not all the walls have dry wall, and one of
the walls in the kitchen is still just 2X4's with clear roofing plastic
stapled to it. Everything in the kitchen looks used and worn, and the
place is dirty. VERY rustic. BECCA, typical American teen, doesn't look
like Sean, puts the groceries away in the background. Sadie is sitting
at the table, arms crossed, staring at Sean as he makes some coffee,
stalling, not wanting to sit down. But finally he does.

              SADIE
    Do you have any money?

              SEAN
    No. I didn't get to my credit
    union today.

              SADIE
    You didn't get to it? Yeah sure,
    and what exactly were you doing
    that was so important you didn't
    get to it? And why do you always
    come home so late? You say it's
    not a plan but it must be because
    you always get home at about the
    same time every night and—

Sees Becca holding a generic multivitamin bottle.

    What is that?! That's not VitaMax!

              SEAN
    They were out of VitaMax. This is
    the same thing.

              SADIE
    It is not the same thing Sean—I
    did research on the different
    multivitamins and I…

As Sadie continues Becca quietly walks across the room to stand
directly behind her mother, then she soundlessly mouths blah, blah,
blah, blah, blah, blah, before pretending to choke herself. Sean
smiles. Sadie turns around to see Becca with her arms by her sides and
an innocent smile on her face.

Learning to be a Good Editor ~ Ava Collopy

                    SADIE
Why don't you go to bed?

                    BECCA
But this is entertainment. It's
better than the soaps. It's
believable.

                    SADIE
Go to your room.

                    BECCA
I'm almost 18 mom, you can't
send me to my room—we've been
over this.

                    SEAN
She has a point there Sadie.

                    SADIE
Don't you step in, you're not
even her real father.

Sean and Becca look hurt by that comment; Sadie knows how to push this
button.

                    SADIE
Now Sean, will you go to church
with us tomorrow?

                    SEAN
I can't, I have to work.

                    SADIE
I can't believe this. Your kids
never see you anymore. You're
always working seven days a week.

                    SEAN
It feels like eight days a week,
and I'm no happier about it than
anyone else is.

                    SADIE
Well the kids and I are going.
Becca will be singing in the
youth choir, remember? I can't

Learning to be a Good Editor ~ Ava Collopy

believe you're not going to be
there for her.

                SEAN
I would love to be there but I
need to put food on the table.

                SADIE
She'll be hurt if you miss her
performance.

                SEAN
Yeah well, she'll really be
hurting if she hasn't got any
food to eat or a roof over her
head. Just take the tape
recorder and the camera.

                SADIE
We don't have any batteries for
them.

                SEAN
What do you mean you don't have
any batteries? I just bought a
ton of batteries.

                SADIE
You bought batteries two months
ago.

                SEAN
Yeah, two months ago I bought a
ton of batteries. You couldn't
have used them all up already.

                SADIE
God, you're impossible Sean.
You're so damn cheap. You just
expect everything to last forever
so you won't have to spend any
money, ever.

                SEAN
I'd spend money if I had any
money to spend.

Learning to be a Good Editor ~ Ava Collopy

                    SADIE
          Then why don't you make more
          money?

                    SEAN
          Well that's why I'm going to
          work tomorrow.

                    SADIE
          I just can't listen to you anymore.

Sadie gets up, leaves the room. Becca rolls her eyes.

                    BECCA
          Don't worry about my performance,
          I'm only doing it because mom
          wants me to, okay?

                    SEAN
          Okay, kiddo.

                    BECCA
          I'm going to go to bed.

Becca leaves the kitchen.

                    SEAN
          That's not a bad idea.

Sean turns off the light, leaves the kitchen, walks into the front
room. He sits on the bench by the fire stove, feeds it one last time
and damps it off for the night. He checks that there's dry kindling for
tomorrow.
He leaves the bench and walks to the nearby couch that folds down. He
sets it up, takes off his shoes, turns off the lamp.

INT. CABIN LIVING ROOM AND KITCHEN - DAY

The alarm wakes Sean at 6 a.m. He gets up, it's cold. He starts to make
a fire and, bending over the stove, he feels a spasm in his lower back.
He cringes in pain and puts his hands on it, as Becca comes down the
stairs.

                    BECCA
          Hey dad, why don't you let me
          do that?

                                                                    31

Learning to be a Good Editor ~ Ava Collopy

                    SEAN
          Thanks Becca.

He walks into the kitchen and starts a pot of coffee. When it's ready
he pours a cup and takes an aspirin with it. He walks back into the
front room to see there's a fire made and the whole area around the
stove has been swept up and organized; it suddenly looks very tidy.

                    SEAN
          How long was I gone?

                    BECCA
          What?

                    SEAN
          It must be because you're a
          female that you can do so many
          more tasks, faster, and with a
          cleaner work area than I ever
          can.

                    BECCA
          I love being female.

She walks into the kitchen and starts making pancakes, as she does Sean
hands her things like the pancake mix when she's ready or the stirring
spoon, etc. And as she makes breakfast they talk.

                    SEAN
          How's the job hunting coming along?

                    BECCA
          Oh… not so good. Not so good.
          There just aren't a lot of jobs
          all the way out here. I almost
          got a job working at that little
          gift shop in that tiny strip mall
          in Damascus, you know the place?

                    SEAN
          Yeah. .

                    BECCA
          But then the manager gave the
          job to her niece. I wish there
          were a video store within 10
          miles of here, then I could

Learning to be a Good Editor ~ Ava Collopy

watch movies all day when I was
supposed to be working.

                SEAN
Yeah, well, if you keep working
at it you'll get hired somewhere
at some point.

                BECCA
Yeah dad, but the job market
just isn't what it was when
you and mom were my age.
Everywhere I go people want me
to have had previous experience.

                SEAN
Ah yes, "previous experience".
That's what we call a Catch 22—
you can't get the experience
without getting the job but you
can't get the job without first
getting the experience.

                BECCA
Exactly! And there just aren't
any jobs out here, so far from
the city. It would just be so
much easier to get a job if I
were in the city, you know? I've
been looking for a job for almost
half a year now and there just
aren't any jobs out here.

                SEAN
You have to just keep chipping
away at these things.

                BECCA
Yeah well, I told mom it would be
easier for me to find a job if I
were in the city but she said we
couldn't afford anything like
that. I said I knew that but I'd
been thinking that uncle Alan has
a spare room—grandma's room—and I
could stay there for a while, you
know just until I could get a job

Learning to be a Good Editor ~ Ava Collopy

and pay for my own apartment and
everything. But mom said no,
absolutely not.

                    SEAN
          Really?

                    BECCA
          Yeah, and I thought that was a
          shame because there are so many
          more jobs in the city and there
          are buses and the light rail so
          mom wouldn't have to drive me
          everywhere and use up all her
          time and put all that extra wear
          and tear on her car. But she said
          no, so that's that.

                    SEAN
          Well, if you think you need to
          be in the city to find work then
          I think that's a fine idea.

                    BECCA
          Well, I don't know if uncle Alan
          would be okay with that, and mom
          already said no.

                    SEAN
          I'll talk to Alan about it and
          you don't have to worry about
          your mother—I'm saying yes.

                    BECCA
          Thank you daddy. Well, I'd
          better get ready for church.

Becca springs out of the room and we can hear her running upstairs.

                    SEAN
          That girl is something else.

Sean greases the frying pan and starts using the ladle to pour batter
into the pan, which is on a burner plate (they don't have a cooking
stove).
Sadie walks in.

Learning to be a Good Editor ~ Ava Collopy

                    SADIE
          What are you doing?

                    SEAN
          Oh, I thought I'd start making
          breakfast for you. I know you
          find it exhausting trying to get
          to church on time with all your
          morning chores.

Sadie looks at him, not knowing if she believes him, then decides just
to ignore it. Sean pours a second cup of coffee and sits down while
Sadie takes over making breakfast.

                    SADIE
          So you're going to go to work
          today.

                    SEAN
          Yes, I have to, the electric
          bill is coming up.

                    SADIE
          Oh, yes.

She walks to the fridge and takes out a loaf of bread, a can of refried
beans, a half-gallon of Nancy's honey yogurt, a can of sliced pineapple
circles in juice, a half brick of Tillamook cheddar cheese, and
leftover cold spaghetti. She starts making a sandwich. Sean isn't
paying attention to what she's doing at first, then he looks again and
starts to wonder.

                    SEAN
          What are you making?

                    SADIE
          I'm making your sandwich for lunch.

                    SEAN
          Out of what?

He gets up and walks over to the counter where she is.

                    SEAN
          Refried beans, yogurt, pineapple,
          cheese, and cold spaghetti?!

Learning to be a Good Editor ~ Ava Collopy

                    SADIE
          Yeah? I thought you'd like
          something new and different.

                    SEAN
          I don't want anything new or
          different, I want old and
          reliable.

                    SADIE
          Oh, really? I cannot believe you!

She throws the spreading knife across the room.

          You never appreciate it when I
          try to be creative and do
          something nice for you! Well
          then you can just make your own
          damn sandwich!

She storms out of the room.

                    SADIE (O.S.)
          Becca, fix breakfast! I'm
          going to the roof!

                    SEAN (under his breath)
          Not again.

He throws up his hands in futility and goes to turn the now-burned
pancake. Becca walks in.

                    BECCA
          Why did she go to the roof
          again, dad?

                    SEAN
          I don't know. All I did was tell
          her I didn't want a sandwich with
          refried beans, yogurt, pineapple,
          cheese, and cold spaghetti.

                    BECCA
          You don't? Really? I love those
          sandwiches.

Learning to be a Good Editor ~ Ava Collopy

                    SEAN
          That's because you were raised
          by her. My mother made plain,
          normal food that tasted good.

                    BECCA
          Okay, whatever.

Becca takes over making breakfast; starts making a stack of pancakes on
one plate for everyone.

          Honestly dad, I just want to get
          out of here. I want to go to the
          city, get a job, have my own
          money, and not have to be mom's
          crutch anymore. Sometimes I just
          want to run away.

                    SEAN
          Me too, kiddo, me too.

Sean looks at the clock, Becca starts serving him some breakfast, which
he eats quickly.

                    SEAN
          Say… why don't I try to find a
          decent burner plate at Finders
          Keepers. More than one if I can.
          That way you could make meals
          twice as fast.

                    BECCA
          Yeah, that would be great.
          Here, have some more pancakes.

                    SEAN
          Do we have any syrup?

                    BECCA
          No, dad. We're out of syrup.

                    SEAN
          Oh, that's right, I forgot to
          get the syrup.

Learning to be a Good Editor ~ Ava Collopy

He finishes breakfast then shaves and brushes his teeth at the kitchen sink. He turns to fill his thermos but Becca's handing him an already filled thermos while flipping over another pancake.

                         SEAN
               Just like a female—you can
               multi-task like a magician.

                         BECCA
               Bye dad, have a good day at
               work… and remember to talk to
               uncle Alan, okay daddy?

                         SEAN
               I will.

Sean rushes out.

INT. / EXT. CABIN PROPERTY / SEAN'S TRUCK / THE HIGHWAY – DAY

Sean drives on the long, one-hour drive into town and to Alan's house.

INT. ALAN'S HOUSE – DAY

Sean walks in and greets Carrie and Barry, who are crazy excited to see him. Their yapping/barking is annoying Alan, who's set up in the living room to practice German and his guitar (a nice acoustic six-string).

                         ALAN
               So you're working today?

                         SEAN
               Yes. And what are you up to
               today?

                         ALAN
               I thought I'd practice my guitar
               for a while, then get back to my
               German grammar. I haven't
               seriously practiced my guitar for
               a few Sundays since I've been so
               busy with my greenhouse and the
               yard.

                         SEAN
               Yeah. You got a good crop of
               fruits and vegetables this year.

                    ALAN
          Yeah. I sure did.

A beat.

                    SEAN
          Well, I'd better start getting
          ready.

Sean pours his coffee into the percolator to reheat it, then he goes
back outside, passing Alan in the front room set up for his hobbies.

EXT. ALAN'S HOUSE - DAY

Sean loads up his truck and trailer with tools from Alan's garage;
tries to take two of everything in case one breaks: shovels, two of
each kind of three clippers: one for thick branches, one for light
branches, and one for details, two lawnmowers, wrenches, a gas can,
etc.
Then he drives off.

EXT. SEAN'S TRUCK / THE CITY - DAY

Sean drives a few miles through rundown, working class suburbia to a
garden supply shop. Sean gets out of the truck and looks down, tries to
straighten up, but his clothes are just embarrassingly ragged so gives
up and goes in.

INT. GARDEN SHOP - DAY

The store has swatches of different kinds of gravel, bark dust, etc, at
the counter. A woman in her 50's with a bouffant hairdo is behind the
counter, this is MABEL.

                    MABEL
          Hello, may I help you Sean?

                    SEAN
          Sure thing Mabel. I need to get
          eight bags of medium bark dust.

                    MABEL
          Okay. That'll be… $25.60.

Sean looks into his weather-beaten and almost empty wallet and pays
her.

Learning to be a Good Editor ~ Ava Collopy

EXT. GARDEN SHOP - DAY

Sean carries two of the heavy bags at a time, loads up the truck. He gets in the truck as it starts to rain.

INT. SEAN'S TRUCK - DAY

                    SEAN
          Damn it! I hope it's dry on the
          other side of town.

INT. / EXT. SEAN'S TRUCK / THE CITY - DAY

Sean drives clear across town to a decent neighborhood and pulls up near the customer's house. It's not raining there. He lingers over a cup of coffee, stalling. Then he springs into work mode and mows her lawn, removes a few dead rose bushes, and lays fresh bark dust down, cutting the bags open with an old Oregon Leatherman multi-tool. When he's finished he cleans things up then is putting the mower away as the customer pulls out of her garage in a nice car.
She is in her late 50's, black, dressed well. This is BILLIE HOOKS. She's holding a check.

                    BILLIE
          Here you go. Now I have to get
          going. We're having a potluck
          dinner at my church.

She pulls out of the driveway then calls to him.

          Close the garage door for me
          would you?

                    SEAN
          Of course!

She drives away as he looks at the check and it's for $109.

                    SEAN
          Wait! It was… supposed to be for
          $139. Damn it!

He tries not to look too angry as neighbors could be watching, goes to her garage to close the door, sees a big pile of high quality firewood and smiles. He backs the truck up to the garage and skims firewood off the top and sides of the pile and covers the wood in the bed of the

Learning to be a Good Editor ~ Ava Collopy

truck with a tarp, weighted down at the corners by four pieces of wood. He smiles the whole time. Then closes the garage and drives away.

INT. / EXT. THE CITY - DAY

Sean drives back to Alan's house from the nicer neighborhood to rundown suburbia as it begins to rain heavily. At Alan's a nearby social club has an event so the music is loud and the residential street is crowded with cars. He has to park away from Alan's house and walk there.

INT. KITCHEN AND FRONT ROOM - ALAN'S HOUSE - LATE DAY

Sean goes to the kitchen and makes fresh coffee. He looks especially exhausted. After a while he sits down in the front room as Alan continues with his hobbies. Sean looks at one of the German books and reads Hoffen, hoffentlich, die hoffnung.

> SEAN
> "Hoffen", does that mean "to hope"?

> ALAN
> Yes. How's Ms. Hooks?

> SEAN
> The same. I was supposed to get $139 but she gave me a check for $109 instead.

> ALAN
> That's not surprising.

> SEAN
> Yeah, but then I found some firewood in her garage she won't miss. That saves me a trip to the lumber mill tomorrow for wood that would burn up faster than her wood will.

> ALAN
> Well, that's a good deal.

> SEAN
> Yeah. I get paid one way or another.

Learning to be a Good Editor ~ Ava Collopy

A beat.

>Say… Becca's been working hard
>on job-hunting for the past few
>months.

A beat.

>   ALAN
>And…?

>   SEAN
>Well, there just aren't a lot of
>jobs out where the cabin is and
>those that are there generally
>get filled by friends and family
>of the owners of the different
>businesses.

>   ALAN
>Yeah, I'm not surprised by that.
>It's pretty desolate out by the
>cabin, or I thought so the few
>times I was out there, in the
>1980's.

>   SEAN
>Yeah, but there are a lot of
>jobs in the city.

>   ALAN
>Yeah, there are. Maybe it would
>be better for Becca if she lived
>in the city.

>   SEAN
>Yeah, that's what she and I were
>talking about this morning.

>   ALAN
>Yeah.

>   SEAN
>Yeah. Of course she'd have to be
>working to have the money to get
>a place in the city to go job-
>hunting—it's a regular Catch 22.

Learning to be a Good Editor ~ Ava Collopy

                    ALAN
        Yeah.

                    SEAN
        Yeah.

They both look towards the grandma's room, Sean's mother's room. A
beat.

                    ALAN
        Well. There's a spare room here.

                    SEAN
        Yeah. There is.

                    ALAN
        Well, maybe she can look at it
        and see what she thinks.

                    SEAN
        Yeah.

                    ALAN
        Yeah. But first I'd want to take
        your mother's things and pack
        them in boxes and put them in…
        in the closet in the basement.

                    SEAN
        Yeah. Well, whenever you'd want
        to do that.

                    ALAN
        Maybe in the next few weeks.

                    SEAN
        Yeah. Whenever. There's no rush.

Sean gets up, returns to the kitchen to wash out his cup and refill his
thermos. He looks at the clock. It's close to 3 p.m. He returns to the
front room and picks up the latest copy of the Sunday *Oregonian*.

                    SEAN
        Are you done with this?

                    ALAN

Learning to be a Good Editor ~ Ava Collopy

                    Oh yeah.

                         SEAN
               See you tomorrow.

                         ALAN
               See you tomorrow.

Sean leaves.

EXT. ALAN'S HOUSE - LATE DAY

Sean walks to his truck, gets in, drives around all the many cars
parked everywhere, drives off. Drives to the Evergreen Diner. Walks in.

INT. DINER - AFTERNOON

Sean walks in to the counter. A beat or two. Cara finally comes out
with a full pot of coffee.

                         CARA (melancholy, upset)
               Hi. Can I help you?

                         SEAN
               Is something wrong?

                         CARA
               Oh, it's nothing.

                         SEAN
               No, really, what's wrong? Did
               someone die?

                         CARA
               It's just…

She sets the coffee pot down hard.

               It's just so hard to be bisexual
               when everyone acts like it means
               you're a filthy, disease-riddled
               slut! And men act like your
               sexuality—your personal identity—
               is just there for their fantasies
               and women—lesbians—act like
               you're a traitor against the gay
               community and that you can't be

Learning to be a Good Editor ~ Ava Collopy

trusted to not cheat on them and
that you're like contaminated
filth because you've been
intimate with men! As if love
between any two people can
'taint' those people!!

                    SEAN
        Uh...

                    CARA
        You know love is love and life is
        hard enough to get through
        without people making it so much
        more difficult with all their
        little rules and their
        segregations and why can't we all
        just be ourselves without
        everyone acting like all there is
        to life is judging other people
        and being judged by other
        people?! I'm just so sick and
        tired of this fucking society and
        it's constant rules and judgments
        and I just want to be free to
        live my own life, do you know what
        I mean?!

Sean stands frozen. A beat or two. Takes a deep breath.

                    SEAN
        All you can do in life is figure
        out what you're going to do for
        yourself. You can't control other
        people and how they're going to
        respond to you and you shouldn't
        worry about what other people
        think of you. If you know who you
        are and what you're doing then
        that's all that matters.

Cara smiles serenely at his advice. A beat.

                    CARA
        Thank you so much.

(With more clarity than she's had before)

Learning to be a Good Editor ~ Ava Collopy

What would you like to order?

        SEAN
Oh I'd just like a cup of coffee…
in a booth.

        CARA (with a can-do attitude)
Well, okay then.

She grabs a coffee mug, the pot, and walks into the other part of the diner with the tables and booths. Sean points to one that's by a heating vent. He sits down, she pours his coffee, and he reads the paper. He gets free refills as he sits and reads the entire paper, including a poem that he reads to himself:

        SEAN

        "THE GRAVITY OF DREAMS

Lying on my back gazing into a sea of stars
Glitter thrown across the universe
I'm in a depressed slump of the city
Where poor people in rundown houses
Lead bad lives with lousy decisions made
This whole area used to be
Farmed strawberry fields stretching out forever
And before that it was a forest
There's still a patch of wild flowers
As the ground refuses to be
Overcome completely
My back is to the ground
Hung there by gravity
My soul strung to my body
While I feel I want to
Cut the strings and fall
Upwards, out into the sky
To fly off into the universe
Freely through all there is
To do or think or be
But I'm weighed down
By gravity, body, earthly karma
The only freedom I have
Is that I can dream"

After two-three hours he's finished with the paper. He's warm, smiles, it's gotten dark outside. He sees Cara at the counter, attentively

Learning to be a Good Editor ~ Ava Collopy

talking with and serving a slough of customers. She smiles at him and he smiles back. Because she's busy he holds up two dollar bills so she can see them and leaves them by the register. He walks out.

EXT. DINER / SEAN'S TRUCK / THE CITY / ELKS CLUB - NIGHT

Sean gets in his truck and drives across rundown suburbia to his Elks club lodge, a large one-story building with an ample basement, and a good-sized parking lot.
He walks to the large building and enters via the side door. Walks through a large billiard room with a bar, waves hello at a few different people, and walks into the basement where there's a locker room, showers, and a sauna. He showers, falls asleep in the sauna, dresses, and leaves looking/feeling much better.
He goes back to his truck and starts driving home. At a stoplight he pours a cup of coffee and puts on a cassette tape of *Hank Williams Greatest Hits*. He sings or whistles along. And he remembers…

FLASHBACK. INT. WHAT IS NOW ALAN'S HOUSE - DAY

Sean, Alan, three other boys, Sean's mom and dad painting a house together in the summertime while listening to the same music. Smiling like it's the first house they've ever owned.

INT. / EXT. SEAN'S TRUCK / THE HIGHWAY - NIGHT

Sean continues driving then sees the silhouette of a teenage girl or young woman with an overstuffed backpack in a rain jacket hitch-hiking.

                    SEAN
          Oh, no. I'd better pick her up.

He drives past her then turns around and goes back, pulls over, and sees it's Becca.

          What the--?!

He opens the door, approaches her.

          Where's your mother? Did her
          car break down?

                    BECCA
          No. I'm leaving.

                    SEAN
          Do you have any idea how

dangerous it is out here?! You
could get attacked and it's
freezing cold and raining—you
could get hypothermia or
pneumonia! Get in the truck and
let's go home!

                    BECCA
I'm not going home! I've had it!
I can't take anymore! Mom and I
had another fight and she told me
again "You live under my roof you
live by my rules" so I said
"Fine, I'll leave!" and I left!
I'm not going back! That place is
a prison dad! We never go
anywhere or do anything or spend
time with anyone! I have no
friends, no job, no life!

                    SEAN
Well what are you going to do
out here?!

                    BECCA
I don't know, dad! I don't know!
But I'm not going back there! I
hate her, dad, I hate her!

                    SEAN
Okay, I was just asking.

They pause. A beat or two as traffic whizzes by in the rain.

                    SEAN
I talked to Alan today kiddo. He
says he's going to move all of
mother's things out of her room
and then you can stay there.

                    BECCA
I don't want to dad. I don't want
to find some dead-end job and
spend most of the money from it
on bills and never go anywhere or
do anything. I don't want this
life I was born into. I just want

Learning to be a Good Editor ~ Ava Collopy

                    to leave. I want to go anywhere,
                    everywhere. I want to hitchhike
                    across America or—I don't know,
                    anything. Anything is better than
                    the cabin.

Sean doesn't know what to do. Then he thinks of something. It will
involve the hardest thing a parent can do: let her go.

                         SEAN
                    Get in. I'm going to give you a
                    lift into town. I have an idea of
                    how to get you out of this
                    situation without putting you in
                    any danger.

Becca stands there looking at him like he's a stranger or something,
not trusting him. Then decides to go with him.

                    Come on.

They get in the truck and drive to Alan's.

INT. ALAN'S HOUSE - NIGHT

Sean and Becca walk in. Carrie and Barry are excited to see Becca. Alan
is making a Marie Callender's microwave dinner, walks out from the
kitchen.

                         ALAN
                    Well hi there Becca. Where are
                    your mother, brother, and sister?

                         SEAN
                    Well… actually…

                         BECCA
                    Mom and I had another huge
                    argument so I ran away and this
                    time for good. I made it to the
                    Clackamas-Multnomah county line
                    when dad found me and convinced
                    me to let him drive me here even
                    though I said I wanted to leave
                    Oregon.

                         ALAN (almost smiling)

                                                                      49

Learning to be a Good Editor ~ Ava Collopy

Your mother was fighting with
You? So, what are your plans now?

            BECCA
I don't have any. But I'm
definitely not going back to the
cabin or sticking around Oregon.
Anywhere here is close enough mom
can do her thing of looking up
where you live and driving by
your home at 3 a.m.

            SEAN
I was thinking she could go up to
Kelso, Washington and stay with
our cousins for a while. Then
maybe she could go to Iowa to see
our other cousins.

            ALAN (smiling)
Okay. Well, come sit down and
have some dinner and then I'll
drive you up to Kelso.

            SEAN (empathically)
Thank you.

            ALAN
No problem. It's about time for
Becca to move on and see more of
the countryside. Remember when we
spent that summer picking
strawberries with our aunt and
uncle in Wallula, Washington?

            SEAN
Yeah, I sure do.

            ALAN
There's a whole world out there
beyond Sadie and her family's
cabin and Becca should see it.
I'll call the cousins after
dinner.

They all eat at the kitchen table. Later Alan gets his car keys as Sean
turns the radio on. They leave a lamp on, walk outside.

Learning to be a Good Editor ~ Ava Collopy

EXT. ALAN'S HOUSE - NIGHT

They walk outside the fence. It's about 3&1/2-4 feet, chain link. Sean locks a padlock on it.

                    BECCA
          You know someone could just hop
          that fence.

                    SEAN
          Yes, but this would slow them
          down considerably. And it would
          make it obvious to the neighbors
          that someone was here that
          shouldn't be here.

                    BECCA
          Yeah, sure dad.

                    SEAN
          Well, I'll see you… when I see
          you I guess.

                    BECCA
          Good-bye dad.

She gives him a big, long hug.

FLASHBACK.

Sean remembers the first time he met her when she was two years old, and other fond memories like teaching her to ride a bicycle, swimming, hiking through the woods with her and one of the dogs at the cabin, sometimes any of this with the other two kids as well, etc.

EXT. ALAN'S HOUSE - NIGHT

Becca leaves the hug and goes to Alan's car. Alan drives off speedily as Sean looks after them. He stands in the street for a moment being hit by the reality of this. A beat.
Sean walks back to his truck, drives off, no longer in the mood for music.

INT. / EXT. SEAN'S TRUCK / THE HIGHWAY - NIGHT

Sean drives back to the cabin. On the way a cop pulls him over.

Learning to be a Good Editor ~ Ava Collopy

                    COP #2
          You looked like you were hugging
          the white line.

                    SEAN
          Yeah I'm hugging the white line
          because I want to get as far
          away from the other drivers as I
          can because they're all crazy.

He continues on the drive to the cabin. Another cop pulls him over.

                    SEAN
          Is there some new quota that
          traffic cops have to make? I
          only wonder because tonight
          alone I've been stopped three
          times for no reason at all.

                    COP #3
          No. There's no such quota. And I
          think you should drop your
          attitude.

He continues on the drive to the cabin. When he pulls into the driveway
Sadie's car is gone.

EXT. CABIN PROPERTY - NIGHT

Sean walks up to the cabin, through the door.

INT. CABIN LIVING ROOM AND KITCHEN - NIGHT

Sean walks in and sets his things down in the kitchen, where his other
two kids BRIAN and DEVONA are; Brian is well-groomed given his
circumstances, Devona is a clear tomboy. They sit at the kitchen table
eating peanut butter and banana sandwiches and drinking milk. They look
like Sean, not Sadie.

                    SEAN
          Where's your mother?

                    BRIAN and DEVONA (competitively)
          She's out looking for Becca.
          Becca ran away again after she
          had another really big fight

Learning to be a Good Editor ~ Ava Collopy

with mom.

                    SEAN
Do you know when she'll be back?

                BRIAN and DEVONA
    No.

                    DEVONA
She left about half an hour ago.

                    BRIAN
It could take her a few hours to
drive through all the back roads
that Becca could go on and to
visit the houses of neighbors
Becca might have bothered with
this.

                    SEAN
    "Bothered"?

                    BRIAN
Yeah, mom says Becca tells lies
to the neighbors to get them to
sympathize with her because she
gets a thrill out of manipulating
people.

Sean's shocked.

                    SEAN
Becca is just very upset about
how her life has gone. She
doesn't lie and she doesn't
manipulate. And she's not with
any of the neighbors right now.

                DEVONA (curiously)
How do you know?

                    SEAN
Because I ran into her on Foster
Road outside of Damascus and gave
her a lift into Portland.

                    DEVONA

Learning to be a Good Editor ~ Ava Collopy

So where is she now?

Sean pauses, thinks anything he tells them will go to their mother.

> SEAN (he's not a good liar)
> She said she's going to stay with
> the friends of some of our
> neighbors who are in Portland.
> Just until she's 18 next month,
> then she'll get a job. She
> wouldn't tell me where exactly
> they were. I dropped her off at
> the light rail and she went from
> there. I really wish she would
> have told me more.

A beat. They resume eating their sandwiches. Don't notice he was making it up.

> SEAN
> Say… I picked up some firewood
> today.

> BRIAN
> Really? I thought the lumber mill
> was closed on Sundays.

> SEAN
> It is but a customer of mine had
> some extra firewood she didn't
> need. It's in the bed of the
> truck right now but I'll leave it
> in a pile by the driveway so you
> can get to it… whenever.

> BRIAN
> Good. We're almost out of
> firewood because Devona always
> feeds the fire too often so we
> run out of wood too fast.

> DEVONA
> I do not!

> BRIAN
> Yes you do.

Learning to be a Good Editor ~ Ava Collopy

                    DEVONA
          I do not feed it too often I just
          like to keep the cabin warmer
          than you do, that's all. Besides,
          my room is farthest from the
          stairwell so it stays colder than
          yours, Becca's, or mom's.

                    BRIAN
          That's not true at all, and we
          don't even have real rooms—we
          have spaces separated by black
          roofing plastic stapled to the
          ceiling and floor.

                    DEVONA
          Yeah and all of you guys's
          plastic catches all the heat so
          none of it ever gets to my
          section of the upstairs. Besides,
          the fire isn't even my job—it's
          your job. I only started doing
          the fire because you said you
          didn't have time after mom got
          you all of those art books, even
          though she never got me any music
          books. You shouldn't be
          complaining about how someone
          else gets your chore done.

                    BRIAN
          You really are a selfish,
          manipulative brat just like mom
          always says.

                    SEAN
          What art books?

Brian and Devona freeze realizing they've revealed something in front
of their dad that their mother doesn't want them to.

                    BRIAN (lies badly like his dad)
          Um... library books, art books
          from the library. I've got to go
          check on the fire.

Brian abruptly leaves the room. We soon hear him tending the fire O.S.

Learning to be a Good Editor ~ Ava Collopy

                    SEAN
    I didn't know your mother ever
    took you kids to the library.

                    DEVONA (quietly)
    She doesn't.

O.S. Brian can still be heard tending fire.

    A few months ago mom said we
    could all go spend one entire fun
    day in Portland together if we
    all behaved good, didn't fight,
    did our chores, and cleaned up
    our rooms. She said not to worry
    about the money because she'd
    save it up for the little day
    trip. So we all behaved ourselves
    very well for a few <u>weeks</u>.

She stops as she hears Brian go quiet. Then he starts chopping wood to
make kindling.

    <u>I already made kindling for
    tomorrow</u>. He always complains
    about my kindling, that it's too
    thin or too thick. He acts like
    he's the only person in the whole
    world who knows how to chop
    kindling <u>correctly</u>.

She exhales heavily.

    I don't know why older siblings
    always think they're superior at
    everything and in every way! But
    anyway. Mom had said we might go
    and see a movie then go to a
    restaurant and then maybe run
    around Lents Park but instead we
    just went to… some gigantic
    bookstore in downtown Portland…

                    SEAN
    Powell's?

Learning to be a Good Editor ~ Ava Collopy

                    DEVONA (with annoyance)
          Yeah. At first I thought we were
          all going to get to pick out
          something but instead we just got
          art instruction books for Brian.
          We walked right by a whole aisle
          of music instruction books to get
          to the art books, and art books
          cost more than music books. The
          art books were $30 used but the
          music books were $18 used. We
          could have gotten at least one
          music book.

                    SEAN
          Really?

                    DEVONA (with hurt)
          I've been trying to learn that
          guitar uncle Alan bought me for
          my birthday but I have no music
          books. Mom just tells me I can
          learn it by ear like some other
          people have but I can't. And I
          can't even try now since one of
          my guitar strings is broken and
          mom hasn't gotten me a new one
          and it's been two months now!

                    BRIAN (walking into the room)
          Two months since when?

                    DEVONA (without hesitation)
          Two months since our last river
          trip.

Sean is surprised how quickly she made up a story and how convincing
she was at saying it.

                    BRIAN
          So? It's cold now. We can't go
          swimming in Clackamas River when
          it's cold outside.

                    DEVONA
          I know that! I'm not an idiot you
          know! I was just saying that it

Learning to be a Good Editor ~ Ava Collopy

was great fun and I'd wished that
dad had been there, that's all.

                    BRIAN
Why would you want dad there? All
he ever does when we take him
with us to the river is sit on
the shore and fall asleep.

                    SEAN (smiling)
And all this time I thought I was
the one taking you guys. I
sometimes fall asleep at the
river because I'm always really
tired from work.

                    BRIAN
Yeah, mom says that's your excuse
for everything you do wrong.

                    SEAN (almost laughing)
Oh, really? Well your mother's a
cynic.

                    BRIAN (rolling his eyes)
Whatever.

Sean peers out the front window and sees their cats waiting through the
cast of the mercury vapor light.

                    SEAN
Has anyone fed the pets since
Becca left?

                    BRIAN
She (pointing at Devona) hasn't
fed the pets yet.

                    DEVONA
What do you mean me? Why should
I have to do it? I took care of
the fire all day so you could
practice your drawing, so maybe
now you should get your dainty
little hands dirty too.

                    BRIAN

Learning to be a Good Editor ~ Ava Collopy

We're supposed to believe in
equalism and then you insult
someone male in a stereotypical,
sexist way that's very ignorant
and...

          SEAN (almost laughing)
Where did you learn to talk like
that?

          BRIAN
What do you mean?

          SEAN
You're 15! Why aren't you
talking like a normal 15-year-
old?

          BRIAN
Maybe you didn't speak very well
when you were 15 but this is how
I choose to speak.

Sean begins laughing. He laughs until Brian and Devona look at each
other.

          DEVONA (like he's crazy)
Um... dad?

          BRIAN (like he's crazy)
What...?

          SEAN
Oh, you're both too young to
understand how ridiculous life
is. And like my dad always used
to say, sometimes you've got to
laugh so you won't just cry.

Brian and Devona look at him, each other, then finish their dinners.
They put their dishes in the sink with soap and water.

          BRIAN
I'm going to get ready for bed.
You can feed the pets.

          DEVONA

Learning to be a Good Editor ~ Ava Collopy

You can feed them! I took care
of the fire all day.

           BRIAN
So what? I've taken care of the
fire all day on more days than
you have.

           DEVONA
Not this year.

           BRIAN
So what, those other years don't
count?

           DEVONA
In those other years mom wouldn't
let me use axes or take care of
the fire because she said that
was for boys so I couldn't have
taken care of the fire so those
other years can't count because
we weren't being _equalists_ then.

Brian is visibly irritated that his little sister has out-argued him. A
beat.

           BRIAN
Yeah, but…

           SEAN (tired, not angry)
Oh god you two! _I'll_ feed the
pets! Go get ready for bed both
of you, _please_.

Sean walks into the front room and grabs a bag of dry cat food on his
way out the front door.

EXT. THE CABIN - NIGHT

He puts handfuls of cat food in the cats' dishes. He pauses to do a
head count and make sure all 15 are there.
He pauses to look up and around at the beauty of nature: black tree
silhouettes with white and gray clouds parting to show the moon, and
stars above (away from the glare of city lights you can see the Milky
Way). A beat or two.

Learning to be a Good Editor ~ Ava Collopy

Then he hears the ominous sound of someone walking up the hill and turns to see Sadie. She looks ragged but buzzed with energy from the drama.

                    SADIE (catching her breath)
          You won't believe what Becca did
          today. I was telling her how to
          make lunch and then…

Sean zones out from hearing her…

                    SEAN (V.O.)
          I know: you criticized, she
          reacted. You two had a fight.
          It's the same old story

                    SADIE
          …Are you even listening to me
          Sean?!

                    SEAN
          Yes. Yes, of course I am.

                    SADIE
          No, you're not. I know when
          you're listening to me and when
          you're not and when you're not
          listening to me you look just
          like you do right now.

                    SEAN
          I'm not not listening to you, I'm
          just tired. I worked hard all day
          today.

                    SADIE
          Yeah, well I've been busy all day
          too.

                    SEAN
          Oh, what did you do?

                    SADIE
          Oh I know you don't think I do
          anything around here.

                    SEAN

Learning to be a Good Editor ~ Ava Collopy

No. No, not at all, I was just
wondering what you did today. I
was asking, taking an interest
in your day, that's all.

                SADIE
I was driving everywhere looking
for Becca—up and down the highway
and all of the back roads—Harding
Mill Road, Eaden Road, Dowty
Road, Springwater Road, Redland
Road, Woodburn-Estacada Highway,
Ammeisegger Road, Judd Road,
Eagle Creek-Sandy Highway, Squaw
Mountain Road, and everything in
between. Then I had to stop and
refill my gas tank, which ran me
$40. I think she must be with one
of the neighbors right now so we
need to go and knock on doors
until we find her.

                SEAN (V.O.)
She can just wind up like a top
and spin. I wonder how long for…
days? Weeks? It's really anyone's
guess.

                SADIE
Sean? Sean, we need to get going!

                SEAN
Actually… I ran into Becca
outside of Damascus.

                SADIE
She was in Damascus?! Is she in
her room now because I have a few
things to say to her…

                SEAN
She's not in her room. She's not
home.

                SADIE
Well, where is she Sean?

Learning to be a Good Editor ~ Ava Collopy

              SEAN
Sadie… I have to feed the dogs.

              SADIE
What?!

              SEAN
I fed the cats now I have to feed
the dogs.

              SADIE
You don't have to feed the dogs
or anything else until you tell
me where Becca is!

              SEAN
Tell that to Sherry and Merry.

He walks to a nearby dog and feeds her, then another, giving them
attention all the while. They're clearly hungry, and adore him.

              SADIE
Sean, you can't just avoid me.

              SEAN
I'm not avoiding you, I'm just
feeding the dogs.

              SADIE
Oh, right. WHERE THE HELL IS
BECCA?!

Her yelling frightens all the cats into scattering and the dogs bark.

              SEAN
She's… in Portland. I gave her a
lift to the closest MAX stop.
She said she'd be staying with a
friend of one of the neighbors
but she wouldn't tell me where.
Actually I could barely convince
her to let me drop her off at the
MAX at all.

              SADIE
Which neighbors?

Learning to be a Good Editor ~ Ava Collopy

                    SEAN
What?

                    SADIE
Which neighbors Sean? We need to
go ask them where she is so we
can go to Portland and get her.

                    SEAN
I-I don't know which neighbors
Sadie… she wouldn't say.

                    SADIE
Well then we'll have to go door
to door asking neighbors.

                    SEAN
Sadie.

                    SADIE
Sean-y.

                    SEAN
Sadie, I'm tired. I worked all
day and now I just want to go sit
on the couch and read a book.

                    SADIE
Read a book?! Read a book?! At a
time like this?! How can you read
a book when my daughter is gone?!

                    SEAN (clearly annoyed)
Yes Sadie, I want to just sit
down and read a book.

                    SADIE
(Gasp!)I can't believe you Sean!
Our daughter is out there
somewhere…

He stands there, numb, at first with normal posture but then wilting,
slumping.

                    SEAN (V.O.)
Oh my god! How long until she
stops talking? I'm so tired.

Learning to be a Good Editor ~ Ava Collopy

He stops paying attention, walks back into the cabin without her.

INT. CABIN FRONT ROOM AND KITCHEN - NIGHT

Sean walks in, throws the food down by the door, walks to the kitchen and gets a cold beer then goes to sit on his couch/bed while Sadie walks in.

                    SADIE
          You're actually going to read at
          a time like this?!

                    SEAN
          Yes. Yes I am. Do you have any
          idea how long it's been since I
          just sat and read a book? So long
          I can't even remember when.

                    SADIE
          Yeah well I never get to just sit
          around and read any books either.

                    SEAN
          Why not? What do you do all day
          that keeps you from reading?

                    SADIE
          You just don't appreciate
          anything I do.

                    SEAN
          I don't know of anything you do
          Sadie. The kids aren't little
          anymore, they do all the chores
          around here, and they tutor each
          other so what do you do?

                    SADIE
          I can't believe you Sean! I'm
          going to go door to door around
          the neighborhood tomorrow and see
          which neighbors are involved in
          this.

                    SEAN
          Okay, that sounds like a great

Learning to be a Good Editor ~ Ava Collopy

idea.

                    SADIE
So, do you have any money?

                    SEAN
I couldn't cash any checks today,
it's Sunday.

                    SADIE
Yeah I know it's Sunday but I was
thinking that since you're going
to cash checks tomorrow you could
give me whatever you have on you
right now.

                    SEAN
But I need money to operate with.
I need gas money. I need money in
case my truck breaks down.

                    SADIE
You could give me something.

                    SEAN
Actually I bought some firewood
from a customer of mine today so
I don't have any money on me
right now. It's really good
firewood though, and it's dry.

                    SADIE
I thought you never bought things
from customers.

                    SEAN
I made an exception to my rules
for this wood because it was such
a good deal: a very low price for
really high quality wood. And
it's dry. And it saved me a trip
to the lumber mill tomorrow so I
can get to work earlier.

                    SADIE
And what are you doing tomorrow?

Learning to be a Good Editor ~ Ava Collopy

                    SEAN
          A paint job in a woman's living
          room.

                    SADIE
          And how much money will you make
          on that job?

                    SEAN
          I'm not sure yet since I don't
          know how much the materials will
          cost altogether.

                    SADIE
          What does that matter?

                    SEAN
          It matters because I have to
          subtract that amount from the
          amount I make to determine what
          my actual <u>profit</u> is.

                    SADIE
          (suddenly calm, which is foreboding)
          Okay. Good night Sean.

                    SEAN (perfunctorily)
          Good night Sadie.

She walks up the stairs. He sits up reading *Transformations of Myth Through Time* by Joseph Campbell until he falls asleep.

INT. CABIN LIVING ROOM - DAY

Sean wakes up with the alarm. He gets up and goes to make a fire. He hears rustling upstairs then decides to grab his jacket and thermos and rush out the front door.

EXT. CABIN PROPERTY - DAY

Sean rushes down the hill to his truck, hops in, and starts it up.

INT. / EXT. SEAN'S TRUCK / THE HIGHWAY / THE CITY - DAY

Sean sees Sadie coming down the path in his rearview mirror, shoots out of the driveway and up to the highway, rushes into traffic somewhat unsafely. He drives to work drinking cold coffee, bored out of his mind

67

Learning to be a Good Editor ~ Ava Collopy

with the drive. Goes past Alan's, past the Evergreen Diner, and to a music shop.

INT. MUSIC SHOP - DAY

Sean walks in and looks around. There are a lot of upright and baby grand pianos, music books. A well-dressed salesperson looks at him, thinks he doesn't look high class enough to be there, walks up.

                    SALESPERSON
          May I help you?

                    SEAN
          Yeah... I thought you might have
          guitar strings.

                    SALESPERSON
          Oh, of course, right this way sir.

The salesperson leads him into another room. In there are guitars, and an odd assortment of other things, like a didjeridoo, harmonicas, flutes, a citar, speakers, amps, spare parts in buckets behind the counter. Behind the counter is another employee. He wears a loose T-shirt and jeans, shaggy hair. Sean approaches the counter.

                    SEAN
          Hi there, can I get a pack of
          guitar strings?

                    GUITAR GUY
          Yeah, sure. What kind would you
          like?

                    SEAN
          Strings for an acoustic guitar.

                    GUITAR GUY
          What kind? We have copper, nylon,
          steel, and plastic-coated.

                    SEAN
          Uh... whatever kind is the most
          common and sounds good without
          being too expensive.

                    GUITAR GUY
          Okay, how about a pack of steel

Learning to be a Good Editor ~ Ava Collopy

                    strings?

                              SEAN
                    Sure…

Nervously gets out his wallet.

                    How much are they?

                              GUITAR GUY
                    $12.

                              SEAN
                    Here you go.

Hands him the money, takes the pack of strings.

                              GUITAR GUY
                    Alright, here you go man.

                              SEAN
                    Thank you.

INT. / EXT. SEAN'S TRUCK / THE CITY / CREDIT UNION / POST OFFICE /
ALAN'S HOUSE - DAY

Sean drives from the music store through the working class side of town
to a credit union and then the post office, pays the electric bill.
Drives to Alan's house. Runs from the truck to Alan's house, thermos in
hand.

INT. ALAN'S HOUSE. KITCHEN AND LIVING ROOM - DAY

Sean runs in and practically inhales the first food he sees: a banana
and an apple on the counter. Then he sets up his percolator, starts
coffee. Notices Alan at the table, eating eggs, bacon, toast, and tea.

                              ALAN
                    What, is Sadie not feeding you
                    now?

                              SEAN
                    She's pretty mad about Becca
                    being gone. I didn't tell her
                    where Becca went because I
                    don't want her driving everywhere
                    to get to her so I told her Becca

Learning to be a Good Editor ~ Ava Collopy

told me she'd be staying with the
friends of one of our neighbors
at the cabin. I told her I'd just
dropped her off at a MAX stop and
didn't know where she was going.

                    ALAN
That was good thinking.

                    SEAN
Yes, but now she wants to go door
to door to our neighbors and ask
them where Becca is. I hadn't
thought she'd want to do that but
I suppose I should have. Last
night she wanted to start
knocking on doors at… I don't
remember what time but late and
I just wanted to enjoy what was
left of my Sunday.

                    ALAN
But she took you door to door
instead?

                    SEAN
No. I told her no. I told her I
was going to enjoy the rest of my
Sunday and read some books I'd
been wanting to read for quite a
long time.

                    ALAN
Good! That's good.

                    SEAN
Yeah, but this morning after I
got up and made the fire I was
still the only person up and I
thought "I just don't want to
hear her talk to me about it!" So
I left without breakfast.

Alan nods along approvingly. A while later Sean sits down with eggs,
toast, and coffee. They look across the street and see two skinheads in
a van pull up to the house next door and start to break in. Sean walks
to the phone in the front room and dials 9-1-1, waits. A beat.

Learning to be a Good Editor ~ Ava Collopy

              OPERATOR
Hello, this is 9-1-1, what is the
nature of your emergency?

              SEAN
There's a robbery in progress at
12026 southeast Schiller. My
neighbors aren't home and two men
with a van are in their yard
right now.

              OPERATOR
Okay. I'll dispatch an officer to
that address immediately. And what
is your name sir?

He hangs up the phone. Returns to breakfast.

INT. ALAN'S HOUSE. HALLWAY AND FRONT ROOM - DAY

Sean and Alan open a cabinet in the hallway and take out old white
painting clothes; clean but marked with paint splatters from many jobs.
They walk out in their painting clothes, leaving a light and the radio
on.

EXT. ALAN'S HOUSE - DAY

They walk out, hook the trailer to the truck, load supplies, then Sean
locks the front gate. He goes to the truck, opens the door and hears
what Alan has on the tape player. He gets into the truck.

INT. / EXT. SEAN'S TRUCK / THE CITY - DAY

              SEAN
Mozart for Your Mind, really? You
think we need to improve our
minds before doing an interior
paint job?

              ALAN
My thinking was that we might
paint faster if we have sharper
minds.

              SEAN
Or maybe we'll just be even more

Learning to be a Good Editor ~ Ava Collopy

mind numbingly bored. Besides,
I've heard that Mozart's music
only improves the minds of babies
but not adults.

                    ALAN
That's what you think.

                    SEAN
That's what I know.

Sean drives them through working class suburbia.

                    ALAN
I've been thinking of getting a
neighborhood watch going.

                    SEAN
Well that sounds like a fine
idea. It's like Ms. Dohring was
saying to us last week, that one
of her neighbors got her
neighborhood organized and did
watches and then after six years
the crime rate had gone down to
almost nothing.

                    ALAN
Yeah.

                    SEAN
Those kinds of things make
neighborhoods more like they
were when we were kids—everybody
knowing everybody else and
looking out for each other. Not
like today where no one knows
anyone and no one cares about
anyone but themselves. Do you
remember when we were kids you
could hardly pick fruit from
someone else's fruit tree without
your parents hearing about it and
crime was so low you didn't even
need to bother locking your front
door? And you wouldn't even think
of…

                    ALAN
          Shut up!

Sean smiles. They drive in silence for quite a while.

                    ALAN
          You're awfully quiet.

Sean looks at Alan as they stop at a four-way intersection.

                    SEAN
          First you complain that I'm
          talking then you complain that
          I'm not talking. Do you even
          know what you want Alan?

                    ALAN
          I was just wondering if with
          Becca gone you felt… Well it
          would be likely that you'd miss
          her.

                    SEAN
          I do miss her but I think she's
          better off in Kelso or Iowa.
          She's better off separate from
          her mother.

                    ALAN
          I agree.

                    SEAN
          Yeah, I was just thinking about
          when Sadie and I were dating,
          when she got pregnant, she's
          always said it was because she'd
          forgotten to take one of her
          birth control pills one day. I
          was just thinking, maybe she
          didn't forget to take one pill,
          maybe she'd just stopped taking
          them altogether and was trying to
          get pregnant.

                    ALAN
          That's what I always thought.

Learning to be a Good Editor ~ Ava Collopy

                    SEAN
          You never said that before.

                    ALAN
          I said it to Sadie.

                    SEAN
          You didn't.

                    ALAN
          I did.

                    SEAN
          I never knew that.

                    ALAN
          She never told you?

                    SEAN
          No.

                    ALAN
          Really? I went to your old house
          and I had to kind of force my way
          through the door and I had a good
          long talk with her about how I
          thought she was trying to get a
          man to marry her and how you
          didn't have the money for it and
          she should consider an abortion
          rather than have a child grow up
          poor like we did. I was there for
          almost half an hour but she
          didn't listen to me. She never
          told you?

                    SEAN
          No. Why did you do that?

Alan looks at Sean, confused.

                    ALAN
          You're a little brother to me.

Learning to be a Good Editor ~ Ava Collopy

Alan looks back at the road as the lights change and Sean looks back at
the road. He continues driving, drives into a nice area of town; a
neighborhood near a rich college.

                    ALAN
          It looks like it's going to rain.

                    SEAN
          It sure does. I'm glad you're not
          drinking Earl Grey today, I
          finally won't have to drive home
          in a freezing truck with the
          windows open to get that awful
          smell out of my truck.

                    ALAN
          I'm going to get some more Earl
          Grey from Safeway tonight so I'll
          have some for tomorrow.

Sean drives a while longer and they arrive in a nice neighborhood, the
kind of place the staff of nice colleges and those on the city council
live in. Sean pulls up in front of the customer's property. He takes
his thermos out, has more coffee, lingers (stalls) over it.

                    ALAN
          Come on Sean, we need to get to
          work.

                    SEAN
          I know, I just don't want to do
          it.

                    ALAN
          We need the money.

                    SEAN
          I know.

                    ALAN
          Like your mother always said,
          "The sooner we get started the
          sooner we'll be done."

                    SEAN
          Okay.

Learning to be a Good Editor ~ Ava Collopy

EXT. THE ASHTON'S HOUSE - DAY

Sean and Alan exit the truck and start gathering their supplies. They walk up to the door while holding step ladders, paint cans, brushes, etc. Sean rings the doorbell. The door opens to show JULIE ASHTON, an energetic woman of about 40 with dark blue slacks, a pink cashmere sweater, a pearl necklace, and a light brown bob haircut.

                    SEAN
          Hello, Ms. Ashton.

                    JULIE ASHTON
          Oh, hello. Well if it isn't the
          Flanagan boys.

                    SEAN
          We were the last time we checked,
          unless something's changed.

                    JULIE
          Oh Sean Flanagan! You are so funny!

                    SEAN
          O… kay.

                    JULIE
          Please come in!

She swings the door wide open.

                    SEAN
          Thank you.

Sean and Alan take their things indoors.

INT. ASHTON HOUSE - DAY

Sean and Alan walk in with their supplies. They begin to move all the furniture, pictures, bric-a-brac, female crap on walls, etc. carefully as it all looks expensive if pretentious; not olde money, new money in a nice neighborhood.

                    JULIE
          What are you doing?

Sean and Alan look at each other, puzzled.

Learning to be a Good Editor ~ Ava Collopy

                    SEAN
          We're moving the furniture.

                    JULIE
          Yes, but why?

                    SEAN
          Because if we don't we won't be
          able to paint the walls, and
          because they'd all get covered
          with paint.

                    JULIE
          Oh. I thought you could just
          leave everything where it is and
          maybe move it over only about
          five inches from the wall. I mean
          that would be so much easier for
          both of you and especially for
          me, don't you think?

Sean and Alan share a look of disbelief.

                    SEAN
          No, you see we need room to move
          around in. Room to move our arms
          and the paintbrushes… and the
          ladders. Okay, Ms. Ashton?

                    JULIE
          Oh, well, okay. And Sean, Alan,
          you don't have to call me (she
          says this with "air quote" hand
          gestures) "Ms. Ashton", "Julie"
          will do just fine okay boys?"

                    SEAN and ALAN
          Okay.

They smile and return to the job. They try to move everything to the
center of the room but don't want her watching them do it. She leaves
the room soon. After everything is in the center of the room they cover
it all in old bed sheets used as drop cloths. Then they hear a
different woman.

                    WOMAN (JOAN ASHTON)
          Oh my, what are you doing?

Learning to be a Good Editor ~ Ava Collopy

They turn around and see a woman, JOAN ASHTON, about 70, with a short poodle haircut and a red velour tracksuit.

                    SEAN
          We're getting ready to paint.

                    JOAN ASHTON
          Oh you are? That's today? I
          didn't know that was today, I
          thought that was on Tuesday. Why
          are you here so early?

                    SEAN
          We're not early. We always
          planned to be here on Monday.

                    JOAN ASHTON
          Oh, well okay. I'm Ms. Ashton,
          but you can call me Joan, and
          who are you two boys?

                    SEAN
          I'm Sean Flanagan and this is my
          cousin Alan.

                    ALAN (polite but impatient)
          Hi.

                    JOAN ASHTON
          Well it's nice to meet you boys.
          I'll go make some tea for you.

She turns and power-walks out of the front room through the swinging door into the kitchen before Sean can say that's not necessary. Julie walks into the room with some old, worn bed sheets with pink floral patterns on them.

                    JULIE (like a girl to a daddy)
          I have some drop cloths.

                    SEAN
          Oh, that's okay, we've got plenty
          of drop cloths, thanks though.

                    JULIE
          Okay, but I'm just going to leave

Learning to be a Good Editor ~ Ava Collopy

these here on the floor in the
hallway in case you need them.

                SEAN
Thank you. Thanks.

They set their ladders, etc. up on opposite ends of the front room so
they can both paint right (they're right-handed) and each do half. They
put drop clothes under both ladders/work spaces. The paint is white:
they're painting a white living room white. It was painted with a matte
finish before and now they're doing a semi-gloss.
Joan walks in with a fancy tea set.

                JOAN
Oh my, there's nowhere to sit.
And I thought it would be nice
to have a cup of tea and share
some conversation before you got
to work.

Sean and Alan share a look; they don't want to get hung up by this
female craziness.

                SEAN
That's very generous of you, but
we really couldn't impose like
that.

                JOAN
Oh you silly boys, it's no
imposition, none at all. Come,
come, you must have tea.

Sean and Alan are like two boys trapped into submission and go with her
into the kitchen. She sets down the fancy tea set and serves them two
cups.

                JOAN
Now, how many sugars would you
boys like?

             SEAN and ALAN
Oh none for me, thanks.

                JOAN
Ahh (gasps). No sugars in your
tea? No sugars. No—you must have

79

Learning to be a Good Editor ~ Ava Collopy

```
                    sugars in your tea!

Sean and Alan stare wide-eyed at Joan for a moment.

                    SEAN (reluctantly)
          Okay, just one.

                    ALAN (annoyed)
          Just one for me, thanks.

                    JOAN
          Okay! (Like she's watching
          little kids) one sugar for you.
          And one sugar for you.

They wait for the tea to cool; Sean and Alan blow on their cups and put
teaspoons in them to cool the tea faster. Sean cringes when he hears
the front door open and close. A woman and a teen girl, her daughter,
come into the kitchen with shopping bags. They are BETH ASHTON and LEXI
ASHTON, the woman in her late 30's wearing a pink dress with a thick
patent leather black belt and the girl in her mid teens wearing dark
blue jeans and a black T-shirt, walk into the kitchen with some
groceries. Beth is Julie's sister.

                    WOMAN (BETH ASHTON)
          Well hello there mom!

                    JOAN
          Hello Beth! How was shopping?!

                    BETH
          Shopping was good! They had all
          kinds of tempting platters at
          Trader Joe's and I just had to
          get them! Look at this one.

Pulls a small circular clear plastic package out of one of the shopping
bags.

          Isn't it so cute? Just look at
          the tiny olives and onions.

                    JOAN
          Oh those are cute.

Joan gets up, goes to the counter to look closer. The teen girl leans
away and rolls her eyes rebelliously. Sean notices, looks away, smiles.
```

Learning to be a Good Editor ~ Ava Collopy

                    JOAN
          And it only cost $20. Can you
          believe it?

                    SEAN (whispers to Alan)
          I can't believe it.

Alan nods "yes" with an irritated look.

                    BETH
          And look at this platter—it's
          pink!

                    JOAN
          Oh I love pink. What is it
          though?

                    BETH
          Oh some shrimp thing.

                    JOAN
          Oh I don't like shrimp. But I'd
          still serve it to guests, it's
          so cute.

                    BETH
          Isn't it cute? Just look at the
          little shrimpies!

Julie walks into the kitchen with a baby wrapped in a lace-trimmed
light pink blanket.

                    JOAN
          Oh look it's little baby Lucy!

                    JULIE
          Yeah, Tina said I could have her
          for the day.

                    JOAN
          How is Tina?

                    JULIE
          Oh, she's fine.

                    BETH

Learning to be a Good Editor ~ Ava Collopy

Lexi (to the teen girl), would
you like to help take care of
baby Lucy? It would be good
practice for when you have a
baby some day.

                LEXI
I've got homework to do.

Lexi practically runs out of the room.

                JULIE
You know I always wanted a baby,
but Charlie never wanted to, so
he just up and left me. He said
we should have talked about it
before getting married.

                JOAN
Oh that Charlie was such a
selfish bastard.

                JULIE
Yes he was, kind of like your
Luke Beth.

                BETH
Yeah, I know. We had one
beautiful child together and
then he just went out and got a
vasectomy—just like that. He said
I lied about taking The Pill so
he couldn't trust me anymore. He
didn't discuss it with me or
anything.

                JOAN
The nerve of that guy. As if he
had the right to just have that
done to his own body without
talking to his wife about it
first. You know I always wanted
to have more children but then
your father killed himself—that
bum! I loved him though. I can't
wait until Lexi's old enough to
start having babies.

Learning to be a Good Editor ~ Ava Collopy

                    JULIE
          Yeah, she's getting straight A's
          in school. Even in the shop class
          she absolutely forced me to let
          her take. Her father always helps
          her with those projects and her
          science projects, so she'll be
          able to get into a good college
          where I'm sure she'll meet some
          young professor and...

Sean and Alan finish their tea and quietly sneak out of the room. Back
in the front room Sean turns off the heat and they open the doors and
windows to let air in. Then they close all, hang a sheet over the
hallway, stand on their ladders, get ready to paint. Julie walks in
with the baby.

                    JULIE
          Wow, it got cold in here. I'd
          better turn up the heat.

                    SEAN
          No, if it's warm in here the
          paint fumes will just about kill
          us off. And by the way, you
          shouldn't have a baby in here.
          The paint fumes could cause brain
          damage to an infant.

                    JULIE
          Oh, really?

                    SEAN
          Yeah.

                    JULIE
          Oh, okay. I guess I'll take her
          down the hall to my bedroom.
          That's where I put all the
          diapers and everything anyway.

Julie walks over to the opening to the hallway, covered with a sheet.
She stares at the sheet for a long time.

                    SEAN
          Just go around it.

Learning to be a Good Editor ~ Ava Collopy

                    JULIE
          Oh, okay.

She went past the sheet and Sean could hear her walk down the hallway
and open and close a door. He and Alan sigh heavily with exhaustion.
Then, finally, they're able to begin painting. Joan and Beth walk out
from the kitchen. Beth is holding a pen and paper.

                    JOAN
          Oh it's cold in here! I'd better
          turn up the heat.

                    SEAN
          No, no, it needs to be cool in
          here or the paint fumes will
          wipe us out.

                    JOAN
          Oh, really? Well I didn't know
          that. Hey, do you boys have any
          kids?

                    ALAN
          He does, I don't. I have hobbies
          and projects.

                    BETH
          What are their names?

                    SEAN (confused)
          Uh…

                    BETH
          We're trying to come up with
          good baby names for all of us
          for later.

                    SEAN
          Oh… Rebecca, Brian, and Devona.

Beth writes this down as if it's crucially important.

                    BETH
          Okay, and what are their middle
          names?

Learning to be a Good Editor ~ Ava Collopy

                    SEAN
        Uh… uh… I can't remember anymore.

                    JOAN
        You can't remember? I can't
        believe you can't remember your
        own children's middle names.
        That is so typical of a man.

She turns around and marches back to the kitchen, Beth follows. Sean
shrugs his shoulders and returns to painting.
About an hour later (show passage of time through finished painting)
Julie re-emerges from the hallway, walks through the front room, and
into the kitchen.

                    JULIE O.S.
                    (forced, excited)
        Hey, look at what time it is!

Joan emerges from the kitchen with a grin on her face and power-walks
to the hallway. She soon re-emerges with Lexi in tow, and Lexi's
clearly unhappy. Joan and Lexi walk into the kitchen.

                    JULIE O.S.
                    (forced, disturbingly cheerful)
        Okay, what shall we cook for
        dinner?!

The baby starts crying and Julie rushes out of the kitchen and back
down the hallway to it. Sean hears a door open and close. A while later
Beth emerges from the kitchen and goes out the front door. About an
hour later she returns with some more groceries and walks them into the
kitchen with a grin on her face.
Lexi nearly runs back to her room down the hall. Beth walks to Lexi's
room, opens the door, and you can hear something like Alanis
Morissette's *Jagged Little Pill* playing.

                    BETH O.S. (forced, cheerful)
        Honey, it's time to help us make
        lunch and dinner!

                    LEXI O.S.
        I have homework to do mom. I
        should have been in school
        today—I'm not really sick
        anymore.

Learning to be a Good Editor ~ Ava Collopy

                    BETH
Honey, Dr. Fleckenstein said we
should all do some things
together as a family. So get your
little butt together and get into
the kitchen at once!

                    LEXI
NO!

                    BETH
We need to follow Franka
Fleckenstein's advice! What are
you trying to do—tear this
family apart?!

                    BETH
No, mom, I just don't care about
cooking. That's all.

                    BETH
Yeah well what are you going to
do when you have a husband some
day?

                    LEXI
Tell him to cook for himself or
run home to his mommy!

                    BETH
Oh, yeah? Well what about when
you're a mommy some day?

                    LEXI
I'm never going to have children!

                    BETH
Oh, you will! You're a female and
you will want to, you just wait
and see!

                    LEXI
I'm going to have a tubal ligation
and be sterile by choice!

                    BETH
Ahh! (Gasps) How do you even know

Learning to be a Good Editor ~ Ava Collopy

what that is?!

>   LEXI
>   Aunt Jeanie, she had one and she's
>   happy.

>   BETH
>   You will not be like your dad's
>   sister!

>   LEXI
>   I'll be whoever I want to be!

>   BETH
>   Alexandria Eliana Ashton!

>   LEXI
>   Elizabeth Alexandria Ashton!

>   BETH
>   You are grounded young lady!

Beth slams the door and stomps back to the kitchen.

>   BETH O.S.
>   Lexi is being a bitch again.

Sean can hear Beth, Joan, and Julie chattering about this indiscernibly
O.S. An hour later Joan springs out of the kitchen.

>   JOAN
>   Lunch is ready!

Sean and Alan both drop their paintbrushes on their drop cloths and
almost fall off their ladders from the surprise of her sudden
announcement.

>   SEAN (catching his breath)
>   Really?

>   JOAN
>   Come on boys it's time to eat!
>   Come on!

>   SEAN
>   Oh, that's okay Joan, we'd really
>   hate to impose like that and…

Learning to be a Good Editor ~ Ava Collopy

                    JOAN
        Oh it's no imposition. It's no
        imposition at all. Come on, boys!

Sean and Alan sigh and their postures wilt into submission. As they
enter the kitchen Beth leaves and quickly returns with Lexi in tow.
Beth stands back from the table with her arms crossed over her chest
while she tensely watches Lexi set six places at the table. Then she
joins Beth, Julie, and Joan in putting the bowls of soup, entrée and
dip trays, and soymilk out on the table. Sean and Alan sit
uncomfortably in their chairs and thank their hostesses. Sean gets up
and goes to the kitchen door.

                JOAN, JULIE, and BETH
        What are you doing? Where are you
        going?

                    SEAN
        Oh I was just going to go to my
        truck to get my thermos of
        coffee.

                    JOAN
        Oh, you don't have to do that. We
        can make you some coffee.

                    SEAN
        No, that's okay. I'd hate to
        trouble you, you've all been so
        generous already in making lunch
        and…

                    JOAN
        Don't worry about it, I'll make
        some coffee! Sit back down.

                SEAN (strained)
        Okay. Thank you.

Sean knows most women make very weak, watery coffee. The baby (set down
in a carrier in the kitchen) starts crying. Julie goes to hold her but
Beth does first and takes over. Beth talks gibberish to the baby
including a cutesy way of saying she's crapped her diaper. Sean and
Alan find this weird but say nothing (Sean changed his kids' diapers in
a functional way, not in a way of loving it). Beth takes the baby out
of the room while Julie looks at that, disappointed. Sean observes that

                                                              88

Learning to be a Good Editor ~ Ava Collopy

Julie has reduced status as the non-mom there and is trying to get some status by babysitting.

>   SEAN
>   So… what do you ladies do for a
>   living?

Joan hands him some watery and/or weird-flavored coffee (some fancy designer thing that smells and tastes bad.)

>   JOAN
>   Well, I work for Reed College.

>   SEAN
>   Oh, really? What do you do?

>   JOAN
>   I'm an administrator.

>   SEAN
>   Oh, an administrator. So what
>   exactly do you do in your job?

>   JOAN
>   I act as an administrator in the college.

>   SEAN
>   Okay, good.

Sean has no idea what she does. He takes a sip of the coffee, it's awful. He takes a spoonful of the soup they served with disgusting undercooked lentils.

>   And what do you do for a living?

>   JULIE
>   I'm between jobs right now. I was
>   working as a sales representative
>   for Thomason Automotives but
>   after 14 years I just couldn't
>   stand it anymore so I went back
>   to school and got a degree in
>   marketing.

>   SEAN
>   Makes sense.

Learning to be a Good Editor ~ Ava Collopy

                    JULIE
          It cost me $50,000 at Marylhurst.
          Now I've been working on my own
          ideas for some local businesses.
          I want to do freelance work; set
          my own hours, name my own prices.

                    SEAN
          I can understand that.

                    ALAN
          That's a good way.

Beth returns with the baby, sets her down. Beth takes a sip of soup
with her pinky finger extended, trying to look upper class.

                    SEAN
          And what do you do for a living?

                    BETH (proudly)
          I am a beauty consultant.

                    SEAN
          Oh, so what exactly is your job?

                    BETH
          I meet with women at a salon and
          discuss different styles with
          them and help them to find the
          right look for them. Something
          that will bring out their natural
          beauty.

                    SEAN
          Hmm, but wouldn't natural
          beauty be how women look
          naturally, without cosmetics?

                    BETH
          No. No. We have to use cosmetics
          to bring out the natural qualities
          of beauty that a woman has, like
          blue eye shadow for blue eyes and
          green eye shadow for green eyes
          or teaching them about skin tones—
          cool, warm, and neutral, which is
          not necessarily bland but can be

Learning to be a Good Editor ~ Ava Collopy

a combination of cool and warm
elements like pale skin with rosy
cheeks which is cool-toned, mixed
with greenish veins which is warm-
toned. Most women just pick a hair
color that looks good on the box
in the store and I have to teach
them that the color on the box
and the color on their hair will
not be the same and that they need
to match the hair color to their
natural skin tone—warm hair looks
atrocious on cool skin and vice
versa.

            SEAN
Oh, I didn't know it was so
complicated. Wouldn't it just be
easier to not color hair at all?

Beth, Julie, and Joan all look at each other then shake their heads
before turning back to Sean.

            BETH, JULIE, and JOAN
Guys just don't understand.

            LEXI
I'm finished with my lunch! I'm
going to get back to my school
work.

            BETH
School work? But I was going to
teach you how to braid your hair
into a French braid.

            LEXI
I don't care about braids mom!
Not African, not American Indian,
not Swedish, not French, or any
other fucking braid!

            BETH
Young lady, you will not use
language like that! Is that
clear?!

Learning to be a Good Editor ~ Ava Collopy

                    LEXI
        Yes mom. Why don't you send me
        to my room for being bad?

                    BETH
        Okay I will—go to your room young
        lady!

                    LEXI
        Gladly.

Lexi smirks, glides out of the room. Beth realizes she's given Lexi
what she wanted.

                    BETH
        Damn it!

Baby Lucy starts crying. Julie reaches for her but Beth takes her
again, holds her while Joan helps with her, leaves Julie out. Sean and
Alan hurry to finish their lunches and rush out of the room.

EXT. ASHTON HOUSE - AFTERNOON

Sean and Alan are at the truck; rinse their mouths with water and
baking soda, then guzzle cups of coffee and tea.

INT. ASHTON LIVING ROOM - AFTERNOON

Sean and Alan paint. Joan power-walks in and around the living room
three times.

                    JOAN
        Wow, looks great boys.

                    SEAN and ALAN
        Thank you.

                    JOAN
        This is great! The last man that
        was here—who calls himself
        "painter Rod"—didn't do a very
        good job. I wanted him to paint
        the white gloss finish matte and
        he did, but it was just all
        wrong.

Learning to be a Good Editor ~ Ava Collopy

Sean and Alan both nod along to what she says, not really paying
attention. Joan does an about face and power-walks towards the hallway.
Sean waits until he hears a door open and close then looks relieved.
They keep painting, through myriad distractions:
Beth puts her pet parakeet in the front room to get a break from it;
Joan, Julie, and Beth go to the kitchen to have a talk and they can
overhear Beth complaining that her Mercedes was already four years old
and she wanted a new car for that reason alone, one complains she needs
a whole new wardrobe because she's tired of autumn colors, etc. The
baby being carted back and forth between parts of the house. Lexi drug
back to the kitchen, later runs back to her room and slams the door.
Later Joan walks in and sits on the covered couch and talks to them
while they're trying to work…

                    JOAN
          …And our plumber Dave just
          screwed up that whole job…
          (LATER) …and the roofer, Jim, I
          don't even know what he thought
          he was doing, I mean sure it
          fixed the leak, but I can see
          sealer residue when I stand on
          the back step of the shed and
          lean down if the sun is out—
          that's just sloppy work…
          (LATER) …and he said squirrels
          had been making nests out of
          Pink Panther insulation in our
          attic—can you believe it?…
          (LATER) …then when we went to
          Peru for a wedding and they lost
          my luggage and they said "did you
          ever tag it" and I said "no,
          that's your job"—can you even
          believe it?
          (LATER) …and the airport in
          Germany has such a long line, I
          just can't even believe the
          inconvenience…

As she talks their irritation level rises. She's mostly directing
things at Sean, so Alan is behind her and eventually covers his ears
and mimes screaming and stabbing her with the paintbrush, which makes
Sean smile.

                    JOAN
          Well, I have to go for my hair

Learning to be a Good Editor ~ Ava Collopy

appointment!

Joan rushes out of the house suddenly. An hour later she returns. She looks exactly the same.

> JOAN
> I just spent half an hour with my
> personal hairdresser and doesn't
> my hair just look so much better!

> SEAN
> Uh… yes. It looks even better than
> it did before.

Alan isn't looking at her, he's working, and says nothing. Joan stares at him for a long time, he can feel it, turns around and looks.

> ALAN (forced)
> Wow, it looks great.

> JOAN
> Of course it does! And it only
> cost me $80. What a bargain!

Joan power-walks off into the hallway and Sean hears a door open and close. He looks at Alan.

> SEAN (whispers)
> Did you see any difference?

> ALAN
> No… I'm about ready to go mad in
> this house with these women.
> These women are just crazy!

Sean begins laughing.

> ALAN
> Shh!

Sean keeps chuckling. Alan looks annoyed at Sean. Rigidly turns his back to Sean and keeps painting. This makes Sean laugh more. Sean turns back to the wall and nearly falls off the ladder, keeps laughing. They finish the job by about 9:30 and Sean stands chatting with Julie as Alan starts cleaning up and packing their supplies.

> JULIE

Learning to be a Good Editor ~ Ava Collopy

> ...And don't even get me started on
> the airports in Germany...

>   SEAN
> Uh huh, yeah, I've heard, so
> about that check...

>   JULIE
> And when we went to Peru...

Later she hands him a check, he smiles, she goes back to the kitchen.
All of their supplies are gone (Alan put them back on the truck). Alan
is pushing furniture back towards the walls, when Julie leaves Sean
joins him. They put all the furniture back to about where it was, throw
the drop cloths by the door. Look around at all the pictures, bric-a-
brac, etc., look weary, look at each other, decide with a look to leave
it. They run for the door, grab the drop clothes speedily, rush out of
the house.

EXT. ASHTON HOUSE / SEAN'S TRUCK / THE CITY - NIGHT

Sean and Alan rush out of the house (tired, sore, but sick to death of
being there), throw the drop cloths in the back, jump in the truck,
speed away. Sean numbly drives across the city, drinks more coffee.
Drives to 122nd Ave to a 24-hour check cashing place by a sleazy strip
club/bar.

>   ALAN
> What are you doing? This places
> takes 10%.

>   SEAN
> Yeah but did you here those
> women? They think every workman,
> boyfriend, and husband is crap. I
> want to make sure this is cashed
> before it can be cancelled.

>   ALAN
> Good thinking.

Sean exits the truck, walks into the check cashing place.

INT. CHECK CASHING PLACE - NIGHT

Sean walks in, waits. A shady guy, maybe a gambler, is cashing a check.
There's a homeless alcoholic Vietnam vet off to the side. Sean cashes

Learning to be a Good Editor ~ Ava Collopy

the check, turns, gives the vet a $5 bill, leaves (doesn't wait to be thanked).

EXT. SEAN'S TRUCK / THE CITY / ALAN'S HOUSE - NIGHT

Sean drives up to Alan's house. They get out, wearily take their thermoses with them to the gate. There's a note on the gate.

>   ALAN
> It's from Sadie, says she's in
> town looking for you.

>   SEAN (embarrassed)
> Oh god! I hope she didn't talk
> to any customers.

>   ALAN
> You need to get out of here.

>   SEAN
> Yeah, if she comes back tell her
> I went to WinCo but that you
> don't know which one—Gateway,
> Parkrose, Gresham, or Clackamas.

>   ALAN
> Gladly.

Sean unhooks the trailer, gets back in his truck, rushes off. Drives to a diner nowhere near his usual places; half of it is a bar, that's why it's still open. Parks the truck off the main street, walks in.

INT. OTHER DINER - NIGHT

Sean walks up to the counter, which has breakfast bar stools, and a sleepy waitress with a tall hairdo thumbing through a beauty magazine.

>   WAITRESS
> May I help you?

>   SEAN
> Yes, please, I need a filling
> burger and a good hot cup of
> strong coffee.

>   WAITRESS

Learning to be a Good Editor ~ Ava Collopy

Don't we all?

She pours his coffee

>   The kitchen is closed but I'll
>   see what's in the fridge and heat
>   it up for you.

                    SEAN
          Thanks.

The waitress walks off into the back room. She reruns with a good
burger, refills his coffee. He eats.

EXT. OTHER DINER / SEAN'S TRUCK - NIGHT

Sean rinses his mouth with baking soda and water.

EXT. / INT. SEAN'S TRUCK / THE CITY / THE HIGHWAY - NIGHT

Sean drives towards the cabin. He's jumpy whenever he sees a car that
looks like Sadie's. In a small town on the way he pulls into a gas
station.

EXT. GAS STATION - NIGHT

                    ATTENDANT
          Hey Sean. Boy do you look tired.
          You okay?

                    SEAN
          Yeah, it's… it's along story.

                    ATTENDANT
          Is your wife following you again,
          thinking you're having an affair?

                    SEAN
          No… yeah, no money, ragged
          clothes—what woman wouldn't be
          interested?

He and the attendant laugh a little.

EXT. / INT. SEAN'S TRUCK / THE HIGHWAY - NIGHT

Learning to be a Good Editor ~ Ava Collopy

Sean drives home, cautious approaching the driveway, relieved there's a blank spot where Sadie's car would be.

EXT. CABIN PROPERTY - NIGHT

Sean walks up the long hill.

INT. THE CABIN - NIGHT

Sean walks through the front door and is surprised to see Sadie sitting on the bench by the fire stove staring at the door, waiting.

>   SADIE
>   I've been waiting for you.

>   SEAN
>   Well why would you be waiting for
>   me?

>   SADIE
>   Come on, we're going for a drive.

>   SEAN
>   A drive at this hour? A drive to
>   where?

>   SADIE
>   Yes, Sean, a drive. We need to
>   go for a drive… around. Come on.

She gets off the bench, walks towards him, pulls him outside. He throws the bag of guitar strings to the kitchen table so Devona can find it later.

EXT. CABIN FRONT PORCH / CABIN PROPERTY / HIGHWAYS - NIGHT

>   SEAN
>   Sadie. Come on, it's late. I'm
>   tired.

>   SADIE
>   What? Do you want to talk here?
>   Yell? Wake the kids, the pets,
>   look bad?

Learning to be a Good Editor ~ Ava Collopy

He slumps his posture in defeat and goes down the hill with her, to her car, which is parked across the street, behind some trees. They get in the car.

Next several shots alternate between Sean and Sadie in her car and exterior shots of the car driving down the road, and the beautiful but dark and even foreboding nighttime forest scenery.
Sadie starts the engine and bolts up to the highway, turns left without pausing to check for oncoming traffic, and speeds off into the black night.

> SADIE
> I can't believe you'd keep me
> from my daughter, and you'd put
> me through all this after
> everything I've been through. Do
> I have to remind you what I've
> been through?! I guess I do…

He's heard this all before, listened to her melodramatic monologues and his exhaustion and irritation show…

> I was raised in an overly strict
> Christian household where my
> mother was very abusive to me.
> She beat me! And I didn't
> understand about sex so I got
> pregnant at 19, by total
> accident, and then had an
> abortion just after Roe Versus
> Wade had made it legal.

> SEAN (quietly)
> Impeccable timing.

> SADIE
> I'm both pro-choice and pro-
> life and this was very upsetting
> for me! I find abortions so
> upsetting! I'm so conflicted
> about the whole issue!

> SEAN
> Yet when you needed one you got
> it.

> SADIE

Learning to be a Good Editor ~ Ava Collopy

                    Yes, and it was so upsetting for
                    me.

                         SEAN
                    Funny how women don't seem
                    conflicted when it's their life.

Sadie ignores anything he says and just keeps going.

                         SADIE
                    So after the car accident I
                    became addicted to morphine. I
                    left and was addicted to heroin.
                    And I abused alcohol, but then I
                    stopped it all cold turkey, and
                    without the support of any
                    friends or family.

                         SEAN (benignly)
                    You can stop heroin and alcohol
                    cold turkey? My brother never
                    quit drinking. Killed himself.

A sign outside announces that they're entering the Mount Hood National
Forests.

                         SADIE
                    And then my first husband joined
                    the Army and then went AWOL. I
                    got him out of the service with
                    one of my letters though. His
                    commanding officer listened to
                    me because of one of my great
                    letters.

                         SEAN
                    Really? Maybe they just wanted
                    to get rid of him.

Outside they cross Roaring River.

                         SADIE
                    Then when my first husband came
                    back home he found out I'd been
                    having an affair with this man
                    from Italy—but I couldn't help
                    it! He didn't understand how

Learning to be a Good Editor ~ Ava Collopy

lonely I was. He chased him with
a knife and I ran, I ran to the
Park Blocks and collapsed!

                SEAN (doubting)
Really?

Outside they turn left onto Oak Grove Fork Road.

                SADIE
And the divorce was so painful—I
thought my mother would never
let me live it down! And then I
was with an abusive boyfriend—he
beat me! It was so awful, the
tension, but people who've been
abused as kids like me get into
abusive situations like that. He
would hit me and not allow me to
socialize! It was so awful.

                SEAN
Yeah, that's funny since I've
never hit you but you've hit me…

She continues to rant as Sean zones out from it, gets increasingly
exhausted and irritated and the road just seems to go on forever in the
dark, with no view. Then they come to a brief high spot with a great
view:
Mount Hood, a few miles away by then, foothills below it, beautiful
under moonlight through parting storm clouds. He's still zoned out from
her and he just gazes at the view numbly. The view quickly vanishes
back into total darkness in the woods and he's back to being more aware
of her, her noise, and being in the car. When they reach Highway 26 she
jerks left and continues with her story.

                SADIE
I accidentally got pregnant a
second time.

                SEAN (quietly)
Really? You didn't learn how that
happens the first time?

                SADIE
And I just couldn't have an
abortion. I didn't know I was

Learning to be a Good Editor ~ Ava Collopy

pregnant until four months into
it so it was too late by then.

                    SEAN
Really?

                    SADIE
Oh, it was just so awful! My
parents judging me—the world
judging me! And he was so mad—
Becca's real father—he acted as
if I'd done it on purpose. Like
I'd lied to him about taking The
Pill!

                    SEAN
(Finally too fed up to stay quiet)
Look—I know your Baptist parents
expected you to get married, have
kids, be a good housewife, like
my Catholic parents expected me
to get a job, a wife, and kids,
then all the jobs left America
and I was out of the industrial
plant. And no one ever asked us
what we wanted. That was life for
our whole generation.

                    SADIE
Oh, you just oversimplify
everything! You men just don't
understand what it's all like!

                    SEAN
Like you women don't understand
having to do the military draft?

Sadie continues, not hearing him.
Outside is snow on the sides of the highway as she makes a mad dash
through Government Camp, right by Mount Hood.

                    SADIE
I sacrificed my job as a nurse's
aid, which I loved, to stay at
home with my baby while Becca's
real father worked as a trucker.
I traveled around with him for

Learning to be a Good Editor ~ Ava Collopy

> months until I was too pregnant
> to continue. Then I stayed at an
> apartment and had to live on
> welfare while I stayed at home
> with the baby. And I planned to
> have a big family with him just
> like my mother always said I
> wanted.

Sean almost says something, then doesn't bother.

SEAN'S POV / OUTSIDE VIEW:
They approach a section of the highway where large areas have been left blank so truckers having engine trouble can pull over. It's high up on one of Mt. Hood's foothills.

> SADIE
> …and then Becca's real father
> just left me, I mean us, and I
> had to struggle so hard to
> survive…

Sean's totally irritated, tensing up, zoning out her continued chatter.

> SEAN V.O.
> Six more years. This is every
> man's life: work hard and bear
> it… just six more years.

SEAN'S POV / OUTSIDE:
There's an open space on the highway with a large gravel area off to the side and cement blocks where there should be guardrail because of a big drop-off. And the highway bends so you have to turn right with the highway to stay on it.
Sean's finally had enough, grabs the steering wheel and shoves it left— they go flying off the highway and down a very long gravel hill at 55 miles per hour.
Neither of them screams; they stare in terror as the car races down the hill at zooming speed. At the bottom of the hill the car crashes into a tree with enough force to knock it over; the roots make a screeching noise and then it falls over. They're hit into air bags, both knocked unconscious.

EVERYTHING GOES BLACK.

MORE BLACK - SOME NOISES LIKE RESCUERS, A SIREN, A HELICOPTER

Learning to be a Good Editor ~ Ava Collopy

INT. HOSPITAL ROOM - DAY

Sean is in a hospital bed with his right arm and leg in casts. His head is bandaged. He's unconscious. Alan, Becca, Brian, and Devona are at his bedside. Becca is crying but Devona the little tomboy doesn't.

EVERYTHING GOES BLACK AGAIN

INT. HOSPITAL ROOM - LATE DAY

Sean wakes from his coma, looks towards the door and sees Alan talking with a woman in a white coat and a woman in nurse's scrubs.

                WOMEN (DR. WENDT)
        Hey! You're awake! Good for you!
        We've been really worried about
        you, dear!

She approaches, he sees her name tag as "Dr. Wendt"; the other woman has a tag for "Nurse Deanna". The nurse checks his vitals, etc. Sean just turns to Alan.

                SEAN
        How long have I been out?

                ALAN
        About a week now.

                NURSE DEANNA
        Eight days. A driver passing by
        on Highway 26 saw the guardrail
        blocks had been run through and
        stopped to check on it. He saw a
        car at the bottom of the hill
        and called 9-1-1. You were
        airlifted here. It was pretty
        amazing. It was actually on the
        10 o'clock news and in *The
        Oregonian*! I helped them bring
        you and your wife in. I was on
        camera for about two seconds!

                Dr. WENDT
        Yeah, it sure was exciting!

                ALAN
        Get out! What is wrong with you

people?!

Dr. Wendt and Nurse Deanna leave the room as Alan slams the flimsy
door, which doesn't wake the patient in the bed on the other side of
the room.

                    ALAN
          How are you feeling Sean?

                    SEAN
          Out of it. What's in the IV?

                    ALAN
          Morphine.

                    SEAN
          That's what I figured. I want
          off of it.

                    ALAN
          I don't know if that's such a
          good idea.

                    SEAN
          I want coffee Alan, very strong
          coffee.

                    ALAN
          I don't think that's a good idea
          right now.

                    SEAN
          Where are my kids?

                    ALAN
          They're at my house for now.
          Sean, do you have any money
          saved up?

                    SEAN
          No.

                    ALAN
          No?

                    SEAN
          No.

Learning to be a Good Editor ~ Ava Collopy

                    ALAN
          None at all?

                    SEAN
          No. Sadie always spends it all.
          I have $25 in my checking
          account—the minimum balance and
          that's it.

                    ALAN
          Damn it! Your health is of
          course my first priority but
          these hospital bills are going
          to run a fortune. I want you to
          walk out of here but I also want
          to walk away from this with some
          of my life savings. Did you or
          Sadie have any money put aside?
          Anything at all? You're uninsured
          and I haven't paid them anything
          yet. If I don't come up with
          something soon you'll be in even
          worse trouble.

Sean exhales heavily. He looks drowsy, he's fighting to keep his eyes
open.

                    SEAN
          Sell the cabin. Just start on all
          the paperwork and leave anything
          here for me to sign and I'll sign
          it whenever I wake up. And Sadie
          will have to sign anything too
          since we're co-owners.

                    ALAN
          You'll have to sign left-handed.

Sean looks at his casts.

                    SEAN
          Right. Where's Sadie?

Alan says nothing. A beat.

          What? Where is she?

Learning to be a Good Editor ~ Ava Collopy

                    ALAN
          Just focus on getting better
          Sean.

                    SEAN
          Where is Sadie?

                    ALAN
          Sadie… was injured worse than you
          were. I'll tell you about it
          later. You just focus on getting
          better. The doctor says you'll be
          here for about five more weeks
          while your arm and leg heal.

Sean looks down at his beaten down body, feels like an idiot.

                    SEAN
          How bad are the breaks?

                    ALAN
          Amazingly they're just hairline
          fractures and amazingly your
          concussion didn't cause any
          fractures in your skull. Of
          course the seatbelt put a huge
          bruise across your chest. The
          staff here thought it was a
          miracle and thanked their god.

Sean struggles to keep his eyes open.

                    SEAN
          What about Sadie? How many broken
          bones does she have? Does she
          have a concussion?

                    ALAN
          Don't worry about Sadie just…

                    SEAN
          But where is she Alan? Is she
          okay?

                    ALAN
          Sean… Sadie didn't do well. Her

Learning to be a Good Editor ~ Ava Collopy

head hit the side window. They
airlifted her here with you but…
there just wasn't anything they
could do. Sean… she died on
impact. I mean they brought her
here and…

Sean is shocked, so much so that he phases out, doesn't really hear
Alan for a beat or two.

…But it wasn't really a surprise
considering the way she drives.

Sean starts drifting off again. Alan looks uncharacteristically
worried.

Get some rest Sean. I'll start
on that real estate paperwork.

Sean nods "yes" then drifts asleep.

TITLE CARD: ONE YEAR LATER

INT. A LARGE FINISHED BASEMENT - DUSK

Close in on Sean, so at first we can't see who else is there. He has
tools around him, is looking at a water heater.

                    SEAN
          The water heater's not working.
          That's clear. But I can't tell
          why.

Sean leans in closer.

          It was working for a day after I
          changed the elements. The
          plumbing and electrical all looks
          good. I guess the damn thing's
          just worn out. That means we'll
          have to drag it out of here with
          the hand truck, ropes, roll
          boards, and I don't even think
          that staircase over there can
          handle it…

                    DEVONA

Learning to be a Good Editor ~ Ava Collopy

I think we should try the wire
idea dad.

                    SEAN
          I don't know...

                    DEVONA
          Well look at it...

She approaches, points to various parts.

          It's between the water heater
          and the insulation when it should
          be between the insulation and
          the outer metal encasing. I
          think when the water gets hot it
          shorts the wire out and then the
          lower electrical panel can't work.

Sean just stands there; looks at her, smiling.

          What are you looking at?

                    SEAN (proudly)
          Nothing. I just can't believe
          that since yesterday you've
          become an expert on this.

                    DEVONA
          I'm a fast learner.

                    SEAN
          I know, you're my daughter.

                    DEVONA
          Don't say that—I hate it when
          you try to take credit for me.
          Like that time...

                    SEAN
          Okay! Okay! I'm sorry. Don't be
          so defensive.

                    DEVONA
          Fine. Can we just try the wire
          idea then?

                    SEAN
          Sure. Of course.

                    DEVONA
          What's the nearest hardware store?

                    SEAN
          Do It Better at 37th and Division.

                    DEVONA
          Let's go.

She leads the way for them to head up the stairs.

                    SEAN
          You're the boss.

                    DEVONA
          Are you saying I'm bossy?

                    SEAN
          No, no, not at all. You work with
          me for 9 months and act like
          you're in charge of everything
          in my business but no I don't
          think you're bossy at all.

                    DEVONA
          I'm… sorry I guess.

                    SEAN
          No, no, don't be. I'd rather
          have a bossy daughter than one
          that would be everyone's doormat.

They leave the basement through the back door.

EXT. CUSTOMER'S YARD / NICE NEIGHBORHOOD - DUSK.

                    SEAN
          I just don't know if this will
          work.

                    DEVONA
          It won't hurt just to try it. We
          have nothing to lose and
          everything to gain.

Learning to be a Good Editor ~ Ava Collopy

                        SEAN
          I can't argue with that.

They walk from the backyard to the front, by the sidewalk.

                        DEVONA
          Hey, let's stop for a minute and
          look at those red bricks.

They stop in front of the house next door.

          Wow, they've really dulled down.

                        SEAN
          Of course they have, she never
          let me put a finish on them to
          protect them from the weather.
          Do you remember why she wanted
          those bricks put there? Because
          she thought the red would look
          nice and cheery and now look at
          them.

Sean grins, chuckles, begins to laugh.

                        DEVONA
          What's so funny? We worked
          really hard putting those bricks
          in, remember?

                        SEAN (chuckles)
          Oh, I remember.

                        DEVONA
          We had to dig through tree
          roots and gravel with spade
          shovels, pick axes, and handsaws,
          even though Ms. Hsiung said
          those trees are endangered.

                        SEAN (chuckles)
          I know.

                        DEVONA
          Then we had to roll the ground
          flat with a water roller full of

Learning to be a Good Editor ~ Ava Collopy

200 pounds of water and...

          SEAN (chuckling)
...I know...

          DEVONA
...drive to Clackamas to get
different red bricks from three
different hardware stores then
wait like three weeks while she
picked just one kind of red
brick...

          SEAN (chuckling)
...and she works for the Portland
Planning Commission...

          DEVONA
...and then her husband called to
tell us how to do our job...

          SEAN (chuckling)
...because he felt emasculated
because she owns the house and
controls all the house and yard
projects. And his instructions
were incorrect, and I already
knew I'd need to put the bricks
in at a slant...

          DEVONA
...with a 2 by 4 cut lengthwise at
a slight slant to level the sand
we'd put down before laying down
the bricks height-wise opposite
lengthwise and then she'd had the
audacity to call us to complain
about the price!

          SEAN (chuckling)
Yeah, but then—do you remember?—
there were four inches of sand
left over at the top. And she
couldn't decide if she wanted it
reseeded with lawn or if she'd
like a border of flowers. Then a
neighbor's cat used it as a

Learning to be a Good Editor ~ Ava Collopy

litter box and she stepped in
cat waste with $300 shoes on!

Sean laughs uncontrollably. Devona starts laughing too.

        Besides, all of Ladd's Addition
        has green lawns and green lawn
        curb strips so this just stands
        out like a sore thumb. I'm
        living in a nutso world, the
        nutso world of my customers.

                DEVONA (chuckling)
        Well, I can't argue with that.

They walk to the truck.

INT. / EXT. SEAN'S TRUCK - THE CITY - DUSK

They drive to the hardware store.

INT. HARDWARE STORE. DUSK.

They walk to the aisle with rolls of wire and cut about a one-foot
section from the 0.12 wire, walk to the counter. The woman behind the
counter, AMBER, is petite but strong, tomboyish, freckles, but with red
lipstick.

                SEAN
        Hi Amber.

                DEVONA
        Hi Sean.

                SEAN
        This is my youngest, Devona;
        this is Amber, the owner of the
        store Jack's new wife.

                DEVONA and AMBER
        Hi.

He hands her the wire, she rings them up, Sean pays as they talk.

                AMBER (smiling)
        I'm not "new" Sean, we've been
        married two years.

Learning to be a Good Editor ~ Ava Collopy

                    SEAN
          Trust me, that's still a new
          marriage. Running any new
          advertising campaigns?

                    AMBER
          Not yet but I'm… I'll come up
          with something, I always do.

                    SEAN
          She's always coming up with new
          marketing ideas.

                    AMBER
          Yeah. Profits have gone up by 15%
          since I married him. Well… maybe
          10% when you subtract the cost of
          advertising.

                    SEAN
          Yeah but any percent is good.

                    AMBER
          Yeah and it keeps me busy.

                    DEVONA
          And it's better than staying at
          home with a totally unnecessary
          baby.

Sean smiles awkwardly.

                    SEAN
          Don't mind her, I've just been
          telling her that she's smart and
          should get an education before
          getting a guy or even thinking
          about having any kids.

                    AMBER (smiles)
          Hmm, sounds like my dad. I don't
          like babies myself. But I love
          advertising. Anyway, I'll see
          you later Sean.

                    SEAN

Learning to be a Good Editor ~ Ava Collopy

                    See you later.

                              DEVONA
                    See ya.

INT. BASEMENT. NIGHT.

Sean and Devona work on the water heater; they cut the wire running
along the body of the water heater, under the insulation, and put in a
new wire that runs outside the water heater to connect. Then Sean takes
out his electrical tester.

                              SEAN
                    I hope this works.

                              DEVONA
                    Let me try.

She takes the tester and tests both the top and bottom parts. It lights
up at both of them.

                    Both panels have an electrical
                    charge.

Sean smiles proudly.

                              SEAN
                    Okay. Then let's pack it up for
                    the day and hope this works.

They start packing up tools.

INT. / EXT. SEAN'S TRUCK / THE CITY - NIGHT

Sean drives them home while Devona pops a CD into the new CD player.
Something like U2. She turns it off as they pull up to Alan's / The
Flanagans' house. Alan's new used truck and second work trailer are
already there.

                              SEAN
                    Hmm, Alan and Brian are already
                    home from their job.

                              DEVONA
                    Oh dad, can you give me a lift
                    to my music lessons tomorrow?

Learning to be a Good Editor ~ Ava Collopy

                    SEAN
          Of course.

INT. ALAN'S / FLANAGANS' HOUSE - NIGHT

Sean and Devona walk in. There's loud music playing, like The Verve
Pipe.

                    SEAN
          What is that awful wall of noise?

                    BRIAN
          It's not awful, it's The Verve
          Pipe, it's great! And they write
          very good lyrics!

                    SEAN
          How can you tell when it's such
          a wall of noise?

                    BRIAN
          Devona, tell him what great songs
          they are!

                    DEVONA
          They're pretty good lyrics but
          the overall songs leave a lot to
          be desired.

                    BRIAN
          They do not!

                    DEVONA
          Yes they do. I wish bands like
          The Verve Pipe wouldn't yell
          their songs at us—they could just
          sing them.

                    BRIAN
          That's sacrilege against the
          greatest band ever!

                    DEVONA
          No, it's not… because U2 is the
          greatest band ever!

                    SEAN

Learning to be a Good Editor ~ Ava Collopy

I like Hank Williams.

                    DEVONA and BRIAN
        NO!

                    DEVONA
        Hank Williams never sang on key.

                    SEAN
        Don't you see? He had a unique way…

                    DEVONA and BRIAN
        NO!

                    SEAN (smiling)
        Oh you two! You're so critical!

                    BECCA (O.S.)
        Dinner's ready!

Brian turns off the music and they all walk into the kitchen, where
Becca and Alan have made a nice big meal. The dogs are under the table
waiting for scraps, treats.
Sean sits back and enjoys a perfect moment with his family.

FADE OUT. ROLL CREDITS.

Learning to be a Good Editor ~ Ava Collopy

Chapter 3—8 Days a Week: the Novel Adapted into a Stage Play

8 DAYS A WEEK
_____

A Play in Two Acts
by
Ava Collopy

Cast of Characters

Sean   A man in his late 40's, wears work clothes,
            which are worn.

Alan   A man in his late 40's/early 50's, wears
            work clothes which are less worn than
            Sean's. Sean's brother.

Sadie   A woman in her late 40's, somewhat
            overweight, has messy hair, has really let
            herself go. Sean's wife.

Becca   A teenage girl who's almost 18, wears blue
            jeans, plaid shirt, boots. Sean's
            stepdaughter.

ACT I

Scene I

SETTING: A customer's property and a work truck (two chairs).

Sean and Alan are finishing a day at work. Sean returns from the customer's yard to the truck. Alan is loading tools onto the truck.

                SEAN
Do you need any help loading
the tools back onto the truck?

                ALAN
No, I'm almost done.

                SEAN
Well, Ms. Barrington is happy
with the work on her lawn.

                ALAN
Good.

                SEAN
I got the check.

                ALAN
It's too late to cash it today
though.

                SEAN
I'll do it first thing Monday.

                ALAN
Sure thing. Let's get home, I'm
hungry.

                SEAN
Yeah. Actually, can we stop at

Learning to be a Good Editor ~ Ava Collopy

a diner?

                ALAN
Sure. But won't Sadie have some
dinner waiting for you?

                SEAN
I don't know. Sometimes there
are dinner leftovers and sometimes
there aren't. Besides, I still have
to get the groceries and drive out
to the cabin. I won't be home for
another two or three hours.

                ALAN
You'd think she could leave you
some dinner since you're paying
for everything.

                SEAN
Yeah, you'd think.

                ALAN
You should really talk to her
about that.

                SEAN
And say what?

                ALAN
Anything that needs to be said.

                SEAN
No, it would just cause trouble.
We might have another fight. I'd
probably wind up looking bad in
front of the kids. That's what
happened before.

                ALAN
How would you look bad?

                SEAN
Who knows? I mean, I don't know
what she says to the kids when
I'm not there. I don't really
know what she gets up to after I

Learning to be a Good Editor ~ Ava Collopy

                    ALAN
What do you mean?

                    SEAN
Remember last week when we
finished very early?

                    ALAN
Yeah.

                    SEAN
When I got home the kids were
there and she was gone.

                    ALAN
Gone where?

                    SEAN
They didn't know. Then she got
home and yelled at everyone for
being up so late, but I thought
she was mad they were talking to
me without her there.

                    ALAN
So what do you think she's been
up to?

                    SEAN
Who knows? An affair? A gambling
habit? Nothing would surprise me.
She used to be fun, then she just…
well.

                    ALAN
Sean, you can't… things can't go
on like this.

                    SEAN
They won't. I mean, next month
Becca turns 18, then in three
years Brian will be 18, and in
six years Devona, so…

                    ALAN

Learning to be a Good Editor ~ Ava Collopy

leave.

Six years? Can you really wait?

        SEAN
Don't really have a choice.

Pause. A beat.

        ALAN
Well, I'm hungry. So diner it
is. I'm paying.

ACT I

Scene 2

SETTING: Cabin front porch, kitchen, then living room.

Sean walks to the porch carrying two stuffed bags of groceries. He
stops, puts the groceries on the front porch, and goes to give the
family dogs attention. After a moment Sadie, impatient, stressed, comes
out of the cabin.

        SEAN
Hi, Sadie.

        SADIE
Why do you have to get the dogs
riled up every night?! And god—
don't leave the groceries on the
porch where they'll get wet and
ruined. What is wrong with your
brain?!

        SEAN
They're under the roof.

        SADIE (mocking)
They're under the roof.

She turns and calls back into the cabin.

    Becca, come put the groceries

Learning to be a Good Editor ~ Ava Collopy

away.

Sean leaves the dogs. They all go into the kitchen, where Sean makes some coffee as Becca puts away the groceries.

> SADIE
> Do you have any money?

> SEAN
> No. I didn't get to…

> SADIE
> You didn't get to it? Yeah sure,
> and what exactly were you doing
> that was so important you didn't
> get to it? And why do you always
> come home so late? You say it's
> not a plan but it must be because
> you always get home at about the
> same time every night and—

Sees a generic multivitamin bottle in the groceries.

> What is that?! That's not
> VitaMax!

> SEAN
> They were out of VitaMax, this…

> SADIE
> They're never out of VitaMax.

> SEAN
> This is the same thing.

> SADIE
> It is not the same thing Sean—I
> did research on this, on the
> different multivitamins and I know
> that VitaMax is the best possible
> one.

As Sadie continues Becca is behind her back and mockingly imitates her, which makes Sean smile.

> I read the ingredients of each
> and compared them all…

123

Learning to be a Good Editor ~ Ava Collopy

Sadie notices Sean looking behind her, smiling. Sadie turns around to face Becca, who's now just standing there smiling.

                Why don't you go to bed?

                          BECCA
                But this is entertainment. It's
                better than the soaps. It's
                believable.

                          SADIE
                Go to your room.

                          BECCA
                I'm almost 18 mom, you can't
                send me to my room—we've been
                over this.

                          SEAN
                She has a point there Sadie.

                          SADIE
                Don't you step in, you're not
                even her real father.

Sean and Becca look hurt by that comment; Sadie knows how to push this button.

                          SADIE
                Now Sean, will you go to church
                with us tomorrow?

                          SEAN
                I can't, I have to work.

                          SADIE
                I can't believe this. Your kids
                never see you anymore. You're
                always working seven days a week.

                          SEAN
                It feels like eight days a week,
                and I'm not happy about it either.

                          SADIE
                Well the kids and I are going.

Learning to be a Good Editor ~ Ava Collopy

Becca will be singing in the
youth choir, remember? I can't
believe you're not going to be
there for her.

                SEAN
I would love to be there but I
need to put food on the table.

                SADIE
She'll be hurt if you miss her
performance.

                SEAN
Yeah well, she'll really be
hurting if she hasn't got any
food to eat or a roof over her
head. Just take the tape
recorder and the camera.

                SADIE
We don't have any batteries for
them.

                SEAN
What do you mean you don't have
any batteries? I just bought a
ton of batteries.

                SADIE
You bought batteries two months
ago.

                SEAN
Yeah, two months ago I bought a
ton of batteries. You couldn't
have used them all already.

                SADIE
God, you're impossible Sean.
You're so damn cheap. You just
expect everything to last forever
so you won't have to spend any
money, ever.

                SEAN
I'd spend money if I had money.

                    SADIE
          Then why don't you make more
          money?

                    SEAN
          Well that's why I'm going to
          work tomorrow.

                    SADIE
          I just can't listen to you anymore.

Sadie gets up, leaves the room. Becca rolls her eyes.

                    BECCA
          Don't worry about my performance,
          I'm only doing it because mom
          wants me to, okay?

                    SEAN
          Okay, kiddo.

                    BECCA
          I'm going to go to bed.

Becca leaves the kitchen.

                    SEAN
          That's not a bad idea.

Sean leaves the kitchen.

ACT I

Scene 3

SETTING: Sadie's/ the master bedroom.

Becca is in the room with a rumpled piece of paper in hand, looks very
upset. Sadie enters.

                    SADIE

Learning to be a Good Editor ~ Ava Collopy

Becca? Get out of my room and
go to bed!

             BECCA
What is this?!

             SADIE
What?

             BECCA
This. I just saw it in the trash—
a letter from Cedar Bear Diner!

             SADIE
What were you doing looking through
my...?!

             BECCA
They wanted to train me! I could
have had a job! I've been looking
for work for months mom—why?!

             SADIE
You're so selfish—only thinking
of yourself. What abut me Becca?!

             BECCA
What about you?! Haven't I done
enough for you?! Helping you raise
my brother and sister since you
decided to start home-schooling
them?!

             SADIE
They have to be home-schooled,
public schools are too dangerous—
they're full of drugs, sex, and
bullying! Do you want your little
brother and sister to get beaten
up—or worse?!

             BECCA
Why would you do this?! I need a
job!

             SADIE
I need you here! I told you I

Learning to be a Good Editor ~ Ava Collopy

didn't want you looking for work
but you're so selfish you went
and looked anyway! Taking up
hours of my time driving you
around to job interviews and…!

                    BECCA
I would have driven myself but
you wouldn't let me!

                    SADIE
It's my car! You don't drive it
without my permission! And you
aren't experienced enough to
drive alone! What if a snowstorm
hit? Have you ever been caught in
a blizzard?!

                    BECCA
There wouldn't have been a
blizzard over the summer!

                    SADIE
I started helping you job-hunt in
March. Now it's October, and
enough of my time has been wasted
on this. I'm tired anyway—go to
your room!

                    BECCA
You can't tell me what to do!

                    SADIE
Yes I can! You live under my
roof, you live under my rules!

Pause, a beat. Becca storms out of the room, slams the door.

ACT I

Scene 4

Learning to be a Good Editor ~ Ava Collopy

SETTING: Cabin kitchen and front room.

Sean is up early making coffee. He hears a noise—Becca is sneaking out with an overstuffed backpack over her shoulder.

> SEAN
> Where are you going at 5 a.m.?

> BECCA
> I can't dad… I just can't take this anymore.

> SEAN
> What do you mean?

> BECCA
> Mom and I had another fight. I… I hate her dad, I'm leaving.

> SEAN
> And going where?

> BECCA
> I don't care. I have to get out of here.

> SEAN
> But you've got no job, no money. Where do you even think you're going to go? And how?

> BECCA
> I don't know, I just need to leave! I'll hitchhike.

> SEAN
> Do you have any idea how dangerous it is out here?! You could get attacked and it's freezing cold and raining. Go back to your room!

> BECCA
> I will not! I've had it! I am leaving dad. I'm sorry.

Becca opens the door.

Learning to be a Good Editor ~ Ava Collopy

```
                    SEAN
          Wait!… Just let me think…

They pause and Sean thinks for a moment.

          Okay, I've got a plan.

Sean takes his thermos of coffee, puts on his jacket, and walks outside
with Becca.




ACT I

Scene 5

SETTING: Alan's living room and kitchen.

Sean and Becca walk in.

                    ALAN
          Hi Sean. Hi Becca, how are you?

                    SEAN and BECCA
          Okay… fine…

                    SEAN
          Sorry to…

                    ALAN
          Oh, don't worry about it. I
          wasn't surprised when you called
          me—that her mother was fighting
          with her. I know what Sadie's
          like.

Alan hugs Becca hello.

          It's good to see you again.

                    BECCA
          It's good to see you too.
```

Learning to be a Good Editor ~ Ava Collopy

                    ALAN
Well, come on in. Help yourself
to the fridge. I'll leave the
paper on the table so you can
check for jobs later. Your
grandma's room is down the hall.
Get some rest.

                    SEAN (emphatically)
Thank you.

                    ALAN
No problem. It's about time for
Becca to move on and see more of
the countryside. There's a whole
world outside Sadie's family's
cabin.

                    BECCA
Thanks Uncle Alan.

                    ALAN
Don't mention it. I'm just happy
to help.

Becca smiles and walks off down the hallway.

                    ALAN
What did Sadie say?

                    SEAN
I don't know… she doesn't know
yet. I don't… I think I'll stall
her till next month when Becca
turns 18.

                    ALAN
Good thinking.

                    SEAN
Yeah, I've learned to delay
everything. Let her wear herself
out whenever possible.

                    ALAN
Sounds like a plan.

Learning to be a Good Editor ~ Ava Collopy

They pause. A beat.

                    ALAN
         Well… make yourself some
         breakfast.

                    SEAN
         Yeah, thanks.

Sean makes breakfast while Alan reads the paper for a bit.

                    ALAN
         You're awfully quiet.

                    SEAN
         Yeah…

                    ALAN
         What?

                    SEAN
         Oh… I was just thinking about
         when Sadie and I were dating,
         when she got pregnant, she's
         always said it was because she'd
         forgotten to take one of her
         Pills one day. I was just
         thinking, maybe she didn't
         forget one pill, maybe she just
         stopped them on purpose.

                    ALAN
         That's what I always thought.

                    SEAN
         You never said that before.

                    ALAN
         I said it to Sadie.

                    SEAN
         You didn't.

                    ALAN
         I did.

                    SEAN

Learning to be a Good Editor ~ Ava Collopy

I never knew that.

                    ALAN
          She never told you?

                    SEAN
          No.

                    ALAN
          Really? I went to your old house
          and talked with her for quite a
          while.

                    SEAN
          About what?

                    ALAN
          How I thought she was trying to
          get a man to marry her. That you
          didn't have the money for it and
          she should consider an abortion
          rather than have a child grow up
          poor like we did. She didn't
          listen to me. She never told you?

                    SEAN
          No. Why did you do that?

Alan looks at Sean, confused.

                    ALAN
          You're my little brother.

They pause. Alan returns to reading, Sean to cooking, for a bit.

                    ALAN
          Well, I'm going to go start
          loading tools onto the truck.

                    SEAN
          Yeah...

                    ALAN
          What?

                    SEAN
          I just really don't want to go

to work.

                    ALAN
          We need the money.

                    SEAN
          I know.

                    ALAN
          Like mother always said, "The
          sooner we get started the sooner
          we'll be done."

                    SEAN (smiles)
          Yeah.

(End Act I.)

ACT II

Scene I

SETTING: Alan's front gate and porch.

Sean and Alan return to Alan's house from work exhausted, rundown.

                    ALAN
          I am so glad to be home. I never
          want to be stuck painting in that
          woman's house ever again!

                    SEAN (kind of laughing)
          Yeah, I could tell.

                    ALAN
          The whole time I was thinking,
          "Won't she ever just shut up?!"

Sean continues to laugh a little.

          She's an administrator at Reed

Learning to be a Good Editor ~ Ava Collopy

College, great, but she can't
even give one example of any
actual work she does. She spent
$80 to have her hair done—who
cares?! And what a waste of…

Alan sees something.

What's this?

                    SEAN
What?

                    ALAN
A note taped to my gate. It's
from Sadie, says she's in town
looking for you.

                    SEAN (embarrassed)
Oh god! I hope she didn't talk
to any customers.

                    ALAN
I thought her car wasn't working.

                    SEAN
It's not exactly not working, she
just shouldn't be driving it
because it needs a new
transmission. She could break
down at any time.

                    ALAN
You need to get out of here.

                    SEAN
Yeah, if she comes back tell her
I went to WinCo Grocery but that
you don't know which one.

                    ALAN
Gladly.

Sean walks off.

Learning to be a Good Editor ~ Ava Collopy

```
ACT II

Scene 2

SETTING: Cabin kitchen.

Sean walks in, sits down. Sighs in relief, enjoys a moment of quiet.
Then Sadie bursts through the front door.

                    SADIE (catching her breath)
          You won't believe what Becca did
          today! She ran away again and I've
          been looking everywhere for her—
          can you even believe this Sean?!

                    SEAN
          Uh… no. Yes?

                    SADIE
          Oh my god—you don't understand!
          She runs away again, probably
          blames me for our fight. Now I've
          spent hours driving up and down
          the highway and all the back
          roads looking for her. Then I
          had to stop and refill my gas
          tank, which ran me $40-so I need
          $40 at least tonight… Are you
          even listening to me Sean?!

                    SEAN
          Yes. Yes, of course I am.

                    SADIE
          No, you're not. I know when
          you're listening to me and when
          you're not and when you're not
          listening to me you look just
          like you do right now.

                    SEAN
          I'm not not listening, I'm just
          tired. I worked hard all day.
```

Learning to be a Good Editor ~ Ava Collopy

                    SADIE
Yeah, well I've been busy all day
too—looking for Becca. I think she
must be with one of the neighbors
so I need go knocking on doors. I
need gas money Sean.

                    SEAN
I don't have any money. It's
Sunday—I couldn't cash checks.

                    SADIE
Then we need to take your truck
and look for her.

                    SEAN
We can't afford the gas. Why
don't we just let her come back
to us? She always does.

                    SADIE
But what if she doesn't? And who
knows what she's saying to people
out there?!

                    SEAN
What does it matter what she
says?

                    SADIE
Because she loves to badmouth me.
She manipulates people into
feeling sorry for her.

                    SEAN
She doesn't… she's just a normal
teenage girl.

                    SADIE
Oh sure, you'd think that. But
you don't know what she's like
when you're not here. You don't
know what anything is like when
you're not here.

                    SEAN
I believe that.

Learning to be a Good Editor ~ Ava Collopy

                    SADIE
What exactly are you saying?!

                    SEAN
Nothing, I'm… just agreeing with
you. Aren't I allowed to do that?

                    SAIDE
"Allowed", like you need my
permission? Are you saying I'm
controlling?

                    SEAN
No, I just… look at the time. I
need to get up early if I'm
going to make enough money for
that electric bill.

                    SADIE
I cannot even believe you Sean!
Becca is out there somewhere and
all you can think about is sleep
and work?! Don't you care how
much this stresses me out?!

                    SEAN
How selfish of me to think of
paying for my wife and kids to
live here.

                    SADIE
Sean, she's probably with
neighbors—that's what she's done
before.

                    SEAN
But we'd never know which ones.

                    SADIE
Yeah, that's why we have to go
door to door.

                    SEAN
Sadie… I need some sleep.

                    SADIE

Learning to be a Good Editor ~ Ava Collopy

>   No, we need to go look for my
>   daughter.

Sean pauses, annoyed. A beat.

>   SEAN
>   Sadie, I'm tired. I worked all
>   day and now… You know what? I
>   really just want to read a book.

>   SADIE
>   (Gasp!)I can't believe you Sean!
>   Our daughter is out there
>   somewhere…

Sean gets up and leaves the room. Sits on the couch in the front room.

>   SADIE
>   You're actually going to read at
>   a time like this?!

>   SEAN
>   Yes. Yes I am. Do you have any
>   idea how long it's been since I
>   just sat and read a book?

>   SADIE
>   Yeah well I never get to just sit
>   around and read either.

>   SEAN
>   Why not? What do you do all day
>   that keeps you from reading?

>   SADIE
>   You just don't appreciate
>   anything I do.

>   SEAN
>   I don't know of anything you do.
>   Besides sit and watch the
>   neighbors with your binoculars.

>   SADIE
>   They're your binoculars.

>   SEAN

Learning to be a Good Editor ~ Ava Collopy

They're a souvenir from the Army.
I never use them anymore.

                SADIE
You weren't in the real Army.

                SEAN
Yes I was. I was in the Army
National Guard to avoid the
draft for Vietnam.

                SADIE
That's not the real Army.

                SEAN
Yes it is, I was trained with
everyone else. What would you
know about it anyway?

                SADIE
I wouldn't know, I don't believe
in war, you know that it just
upsets me. I don't even like
touching your Army binoculars.

                SEAN
Then don't touch them.

                SADIE
I have to Sean. I need to keep
track of the neighbors—they
always act suspicious when I'm
watching them with your
binoculars. I have to keep our
kids safe you know.

                SEAN
Safe from what?

                SADIE
You just don't understand—you're
so delusional! 'Mr. Oblivious',
that's what the kids and I call
you.

Sean pauses, annoyed. Picks up a book up, begins reading. Sadie gets
her coat, grabs Sean's keys, and rushes out.

Learning to be a Good Editor ~ Ava Collopy

                         SEAN
                    Sadie! Hey!

Sean rushes out after her.

ACT II

Scene 3

SETTING: Sean's truck (two chairs).

Sadie is driving while Sean is a passenger.

                         SADIE
                    You know I can't believe she'd
                    put me through this, after
                    everything I've been through.

                         SEAN
                    Sadie, be careful on the turns.

                         SADIE
                    I know how to drive Sean! I've
                    been driving for years and I've
                    driven in all weather conditions!

                         SEAN
                    Yeah, but the roads are icy,
                    these hills are tall, there's
                    very little guardrail, and this
                    is my work vehicle!

                         SADIE
                    I understand perfectly well
                    Sean! And you shouldn't be
                    thinking about your truck, you
                    should be thinking about our
                    daughter. You're so selfish.
                    You're all so selfish—like Becca
                    doing this to me after everything
                    I've been through! I've had such

Learning to be a Good Editor ~ Ava Collopy

a hard life and then she does
this! Do I have to remind you
all what I've been through?! I
guess I do…

            SEAN
Sadie, I already…

            SADIE
I was raised in a very strict
Christian household and my mother
was abusive. She beat me! And I
didn't understand about sex so I
got pregnant at 19, by total
accident, and then had an
abortion just after Roe Versus
Wade made it legal. I'm both
pro-choice and pro-life and this
was very upsetting for me! I find
abortions so upsetting! I'm so
conflicted about the whole issue!

            SEAN
Not when you needed it.

            SADIE
It was so upsetting for me!
Then after the car accident I
became addicted to morphine. I
left and was addicted to heroin.
And I abused alcohol, but then I
stopped it all cold turkey, and
without the support of any
friends or family.

            SEAN
Really? My little brother never
quit drinking. Killed himself.

            SADIE
And then my first husband joined
the Army and later went AWOL. I
got him out of the service with
one of my letters though. His
commanding officer listened to
me because of one of my great
letters.

Learning to be a Good Editor ~ Ava Collopy

                    SEAN
Maybe they just wanted to get
rid of him.

                    SADIE
Then when my first husband came
back home he found out I'd been
having an affair with this man
from Italy—but I couldn't help
it!

                    SEAN (quietly)
I thought he was from Spain.

                    SADIE
He didn't understand how lonely
I was. How much I needed someone!
He chased the man with a knife
and I ran, I ran to the river
front and collapsed!

                    SEAN
Yeah, you've told me.

                    SADIE
And the divorce was so painful—I
thought my mother would never
let me live it down! And then I
was with an abusive boyfriend—he
beat me! It was so awful, the
tension, but people who've been
abused as kids, like I was, get
into abusive situations like
that. He would hit me and not
allow me to socialize! It was
so awful.

                    SEAN (tired)
Yeah, you've told me.

                    SADIE
I accidentally got pregnant a
second time. And I just couldn't
have an abortion. I didn't even
know I was pregnant until four
months into it so it was too

Learning to be a Good Editor ~ Ava Collopy

late by then.

                SEAN (quietly, tired)
Yeah, you've told me.

                SADIE
Oh, it was just so awful! My
parents judging me—the world
judging me! She acted like I'd
done it on purpose! Like I meant
to miss a Pill. And he was so
mad, Becca's real father, and he…

                SEAN
God-damn it Sadie I am Becca's
real father! I raised her! I
provided for her—all you ever
did was drive her away!

                SADIE
You don't…

                SEAN
My life has been nothing but
hard work! You need to stop
feeling sorry for yourself at
some point, kick your own ass,
and get going. And move on.

                SADIE
Oh, like your father always used
to say—you just oversimplify
everything! You men just don't
understand what it's all like!
I sacrificed my job as a nurse's
aid, which I loved, to stay at
home with my baby while Becca's
real father worked as a trucker.

                SEAN
But that…

                SADIE (talks louder, over him)
I traveled around with him for
months until I was too pregnant
to continue. Then I had to live
on welfare while I stayed at home

144

Learning to be a Good Editor ~ Ava Collopy

with the baby. And I planned to
have a big family with him, but
then Becca's real father just
left me and I…

Sean grabs the steering wheel suddenly and steers them off the roadway.
They careen down a long hill and crash. Fall unconscious.

ACT II

Scene 4

SETTING: Hospital.

Sean is a patient in a bed. He's unconscious. Becca and Alan are on
either side of him. His right arm is in a cast sling and his right leg
is in a cast and elevated. His head is bandaged a little. He starts to
flutter his eyes open.

                BECCA
I think he's waking up. Dad?!

                SEAN (quietly, wearily)
Hey kiddo.

Becca hugs him. He hugs back.

                ALAN
Can you go get your dad some water?

                BECCA
Sure.

Becca leaves the room.

                SEAN
How long have I been out?

                ALAN
Eight days. How are you feeling?

                SEAN

Learning to be a Good Editor ~ Ava Collopy

Out of it. What's in the IV?

                    ALAN
Morphine.

                    SEAN
That's what I figured. I want
off it.

                    ALAN
I don't know if that's such a
good idea.

                    SEAN
I want coffee Alan, very strong
coffee.

                    ALAN
I don't think that's a good idea
right now.

                    SEAN
Where's Sadie and the kids?

                    ALAN
Brian and Devona are at my house.
Sean, I haven't paid the hospital
anything yet. Your health is my
first priority but I need to give
them something soon. Did you or
Sadie have any money set aside?

                    SEAN
No.

                    ALAN
No?

                    SEAN
No.

                    ALAN
None at all?

                    SEAN
No. Sadie always spends it all.
I have $25 in my checking

Learning to be a Good Editor ~ Ava Collopy

account. That's it.

                    ALAN
          Damn it! Sean, we need some
          money, and fast. Your car
          insurance might do something but
          that's months away.

Sean exhales heavily.

                    SEAN
          Sell the cabin. Just start on all
          the paperwork and leave anything
          here for me to sign. And Sadie
          will have to sign too since we're
          co-owners… Where is Sadie? How
          bad off is she?

Alan says nothing. A beat.

          What? Where is she?

                    ALAN
          Just focus on getting better
          Sean.

                    SEAN
          Where is Sadie?

                    ALAN
          Sadie… was injured worse than
          you. I'll tell you about it
          later. Just focus on getting
          better.

Sean looks down at his beaten body, feels like an idiot.

                    SEAN
          How bad are the breaks?

                    ALAN
          Amazingly they're just hairline
          Fractures, and your concussion
          didn't cause any fractures in
          your skull. The staff here
          thought it was a miracle and
          thanked their god. As if the

Learning to be a Good Editor ~ Ava Collopy

```
                    seatbelt had nothing to do with
                    it.

                              SEAN
                    What about Sadie?

                              ALAN
                    Don't worry about Sadie just…

                              SEAN
                    But where is she Alan? Is she
                    okay?

                              ALAN
                    Sadie… didn't do well. Her head
                    hit the side window. They
                    airlifted her here with you but…

                              SEAN
                    But what?

                              ALAN
                    There wasn't anything they could
                    do.

                              SEAN
                    What are you saying?

                              ALAN
                    Sean… she died on impact. I mean,
                    they really tried, but…

        Sean looks away, looks around the room, shocked.

                    …But it wasn't really a surprise
                    considering the way she drives.
                    But Sean, just get some rest.
                    Your kids are okay. They're at
                    my house. Everything's going to
                    be fine.

        Becca walks back in.

                              BECCA
                    Here you go dad.

        She hands him a paper cup with water, he drinks.
```

Learning to be a Good Editor ~ Ava Collopy

The doctor's on her way to check
your vitals but she already said
that if you woke up everything
would be fine.

                    SEAN
Thanks kiddo.

Pauses. A beat.

Yeah… everything's going to be
fine.

(End play.)

About the Writer

Ava Collopy has traveled around North America and Europe while working various paid and volunteer jobs. She hails from Portland, Oregon and Dublin, Ireland.

Her work is published in *Adrift*, *Brilliant Flash Fiction* (contest shortlist), *Down in the Dirt*, *Sunlight in the Sanctuary*, *Pulse Literary Journal*, and others.

Her website is Ava Collopy Books: http://www.avacollopybooks.weebly.com

She's a happily life-long non-mom with many friends, who's oft enjoyed being a single independent female, a fact she proudly promotes to remind people everyone is free to be their own person.

Her fiction books are:

A View from the Bottom: Short Stories

The Price of Peace: the Rise of Truthology and the Alliance, a Novelette

Live Boldly, Fear Nothing: a Vigilante and a Painter, a Novel (3rd Edition)

8 Days a Week: the Story of a Working Man, a Novel

Learning to be a Good Editor ~ Ava Collopy

Made in the USA
Columbia, SC
13 February 2025

53743033R00085